ACKNOWLEDGEMENTS

To my family and friends: This book happened only because you have been on this journey with me. You have transformed my life.

To my daughter, Erin Ashley, I love you and thank God for your contributions to my life, this book, and our community. To my late mother, you are my first model for faithful living.

To Stephanie, my sister in the spirit, who said "You can make your curriculum a book!" To Jeffrey Kottler, Ph.D., a prolific author and new friend, who said, "You can self-publish your book." To Jacqueline, who read my rough, rough draft and gave me kind feedback. Special thanks to Etta and my niece Zenobia for taking time to give editorial comments that have made all the difference. Anything missed is my fault not theirs.

To Angella, my fellow author and friend who reviewed my book and wrote a comment that reveals the heart of my message. You nailed it. To Toni and Diane, you have no idea how you keep me going.

To my sisters, Barbara and Ava, who have given me encouragement and support from the beginning. Barbara was my first reader!! Ava created her own Action Plan!! To Malcolm, my remaining brother, live healthy and be well.

To all who will read this book, may you take action and flourish.

To my beloved S.A.C.R.E.D. Women, Michelle, Mt Anna MBC, and others across the country; keep going in the courage, wisdom, and strength of God. May you live Joy, Purpose, Love, and Faith.

Thank You.

At the time of publication, all web links were accurate. Please visit my website, www.hildardavis.com, to see updated references and other resources.

Live Healthy & Be Well - Hilda R. Davis

CONTENTS

To book Dr. Hilda Davis for speaking engagements and workshops, please contact Erin Grimes at erinagrimes@gmail.com.

Book and Cover Design by: Marlo Ross, MarloRoss.com

TELLING MY STORY

Behold, I am doing a new thing;
  now it springs forth, do you not perceive it?
I will make a way in the wilderness

  and rivers in the desert. Isaiah 43:19

I returned to Houston depleted and simply needed to rest. The previous year had taken most of my energy and a lot of my joy. My mother had died and a relationship of almost ten years had ended. I had lived a year in a city where I had no community, with the exception of a co-worker, Danica, who became my angel and my extraordinary therapist, Dr. Clara Whaley-Perkins, who I saw faithfully—every week. I also had an emotionally demanding job and could not find a church where I felt welcome. You get the picture. In the wilderness.

I decided I was not fully living; so I moved to Houston to heal and renew my strength. It took two years and a lot of action on my part, but I had no other choice if I wanted to live and not die (to stagnate, become bitter, or to isolate). I chose life by moving back to Houston. But, it took two years after the move to begin to feel restored and renewed. Healing takes time.

My friend Carla, who graduated with me from seminary over twenty years ago, asked me what I did over the two years to get to a place of being healed. I gave her a brief, off the-top-of-my-head answer. But, as I thought about it later, I realized what a great question she asked. Her question allowed me to name what had helped me "restore my soul." I thought about the past few years and realized the first thing I did was to mourn my former life and who I thought I had been. It took time to realize that my life and who I was before were gone. I also needed to grope and stumble my way to what was to become my new life and identity. I am still not clear on who that will be. I'm sure that will take the rest of my life to know or until it all changes again. But, I do know that something new is emerging, and I am stronger than I was when I arrived in Houston two years ago. I am feeling well or at least, better.

But, I still have not answered the question she asked: "What did you do to heal?" I realized there were three (as a preacher, of course, I need three points) main areas that worked together to allow me to stay sane and well: I **prayed**, found new **purpose**, and stayed **present with people.**

I literally **prayed** without ceasing. I created a prayer wall and prayed for others, too. I continued my practice of reading my Bible daily and I walked. People would ask me how far I walked or how many miles I walked. I did not know. I would answer, "I am walking to keep myself sane--mentally and emotionally healthy. The physical health is extra!" I prayed while I walked. I prayed in the morning. I prayed at night. My constant prayer was brief: "Thank you, Lord." Prayer was at the foundation of my healing.

I also found a **purpose**, a way of serving that is important to me. I volunteered at my church and with organizations that educated the community on faith and health. I attended mental health events to stay current in my field of counseling. I ran around the Houston community making connections—enjoying learning new people, and identifying new community resources.

Then, I stopped. All of that became too much. I wasn't really healing; I was spending too much time being busy. I rested and began to prioritize how I spent my time. I focused on what was most meaningful and brought the most satisfaction and said, "No" to the rest. I found my purpose by learning what did not work—trying to do it all—and doing more of what did work: Staying focused, getting still, and spending time in self-care. I listened for what mattered—healing. I also listened for "what next" – and what aligned with my purpose. When I listened, I began writing this book.

Finally, I stayed connected to people. I spent lots of time with my daughter, with Diane and her family, and with Dr. Barbara's loving group at church where I would go and be received with love and care. I can easily "keep myself to myself" if I am not careful. I read a lot, so it's easy for me to sit and read or take long walks while listening to audiobooks and feel like I'm okay. But, my renewal came because I did a "new thing." I connected with a loving church and community who could deposit love into me without a lot of demands. They contributed to my flourishing. The church group introduced me to the Daniel Fast that helped me eat better during my time of healing. My daughter and Diane were always ready to spend time with me and feed my spirit. I stayed connected to my lifelines: My family in Detroit and my loving friends in Nashville and Houston. I found emotional, physical, and spiritual healing through **prayer**, **purpose**, and **people**.

Live Healthy and Be Well offers you a similar experience to my own healing and renewal. It offers you a space where you can connect to God and to your purpose, through prayer and meditation and hear the stories of other women who will inspire and heal you. You may not have had a major upheaval in your life; your goal may be to create a plan to eat better or learn to prioritize. Or you may need clarity on your purpose at this point in your life. This book is also for you. On your way to changing your health behaviors, I hope you will also experience a change in wellness; that is, how you look at your purpose and what brings you joy.

If you have had some challenging life changes, I hope you will take this time to stop and restore your whole self. All of us can benefit from hearing some good news. It is hard to eat better, exercise, or have energy when your spirit is drained, depleted, and worn out. This book reminds you to get your heart, spirit, and mind together; then, you can make your body healthier.

I pray you will feel the love poured into *Live Healthy and Be Well*. I want to share my passion for guiding other women into living abundantly. I want you to benefit from what I have learned over 20 years through personal experience, academic training, and from listening to the stories of women on their journey to wellness. Know that as you walk this path to health and wellness, you are walking with women around the country who are living healthier because they created a wellness action plan. You can *Live Healthy and Be Well* by treating yourselves with kindness, compassion, and love—as God intends.

God is calling you to respond in a new way. Use this time to listen to the desires of your heart. God placed them in your heart and wants you to be satisfied with good things all of your life. (Psalm 103:5) Create your path to Well-Being and Joy by creating your Action Plan!

Live Healthy & Be Well - Hilda R. Davis

WHY S.A.C.R.E.D.?

Live Healthy and Be Well is an action book. All of the parts are designed for you to think and do something differently. The stories inspire you to love yourself and to enjoy healthy relationships. The activities offer opportunities to practice body, mind, and spirit health; while the meditations give you daily affirmations to become part of your health consciousness. *Live Healthy and Be Well* is a book that will motivate and encourage you to make healthy decisions for optimal living.

This book uses the letters of S.A.C.R.E.D. as the theme of the book because regardless of your story, sacred defines who you are. You may think your story is not important or not worth telling, but God takes your story and uses it to make you strong and to open your heart to God's love and self-love. As you make the connection between your story and God's plan for your life your past life takes on new meaning. You recognize that God uses all parts of your life as a way of bringing you into relationship with God. Your story is not an accident. It is a reminder that God chose you (John 15:16) and nothing can separate you from the heart of God.

So what is the significance of each letter in S.A.C.R.E.D? Each letter relates to a strength. Let me define each of the strengths in S.A.C.R.E.D.

S   SPIRITUALITY

The spirit of God has made me,
and the breath of the Almighty gives me life. Job 33:4

God breathed the Holy Spirit into all of us. God's breath of life and spirit is our gift from birth. When we breathed air for the first time, we received life and spirit—the Spirit of God. The song says, "Spirit of the Living God fall fresh on me." The Spirit of God is as close to you as your breath.

Living as spirit is at the core of what it means to *Live Healthy and Be Well*. Living by the spirit means you can connect to God's Spirit as easily as breathing. Breathe in God's spiritual gifts of love, joy, peace, patience, kindness, generosity, faithfulness, gentleness, and self-control. Breathe out fear, shame, guilt, loneliness, lack, strife, and anger. Keeping your spirit open to the Spirit of God is spirituality and is the basis for living well.

A   ACTIVATES (ACTION)

Take action, for it is your duty, and we are with you; be strong, and do it.
Ezra 10:4

Action is the next strength of a SACRED Woman. Taking action does not mean that you are not afraid, tired, or hungry. According to this quote, attributed to Harriet Tubman, "If you are tired, keep going; if you are scared, keep going; if you are hungry, keep going; if you want to taste freedom, keep going." Action leads to the freedom found in believing you are capable of great accomplishments—if you keep going. Sometimes, it is enough to think about taking action. The thought of a new way of living will lead to taking the action. Dream of making changes in your life, create a plan, and then take action. Get help when you need it (this book encourages you to invite others), but "keep going." Taking action is an important part of following God's will for your life.

C   CREATIVITY

For we are what he has made us, created in Christ Jesus for good works, which God prepared beforehand to be our way of life. Ephesians 2:10

We were created to create good works. That means that you cannot say that you are not creative. I was in a Bible study and the leader brought to the group an art project using family photographs. While describing the art we created with the family photos, we also talked about our lives. Some women jumped into it with joy and excitement—eager to share what their art expressed. A few women hung back and dutifully completed their art, but declared themselves "not creative." Ladies, we are all creative.

A 30-year-old colleague of mine has a wonderful blog, *Unbelievably Human: Love For Self, Others, & Life, With a Twist; Heart Expression is our Medium!* http://www.unbelievablyhuman.com. On her website, she reminds us that using our creativity is not only self-expression, but it is self-love. As you *Live Healthy and Be Well*, you will celebrate your self-expression whether it is writing lovely notes, cooking beautiful and delicious meals, bringing out the best in others, or pulling together divine outfits that scream "Diva!" God created you to create good works. Allow yourself to feel the fun when you create.

R   RENEWAL

Do not be conformed to this world, but be transformed by the renewing of your minds, so that you may discern what is the will of God—what is good and acceptable and perfect. Romans 12:2

What would it take to make you feel renewed? A beach vacation (that is how I renew), a long bath filled with luscious scents, or changing your health practices one day at a time? Whatever you think it takes to feel renewed, it begins with renewing your mind and aligning your will with God's will for your life.

At the beginning of each chapter of *Live Healthy and Be Well*, there is a prayer. The prayer invites the presence of God and it also seeks the will of God for your Self-Care Action Plan. Generally, you decide what you want to change, what it will take, and when this change should happen— NOW God. But, when your mind is renewed and aligned to the will of God, your "right now" shifts to "God's time." It is then that you can relax and be renewed because you trust your change to God. All is well.

E   EMPOWERMENT

Now to him who by the power at work within us is able to accomplish abundantly far more than all we can ask or imagine. . . Ephesians 3:20

God's power, at work in you, empowers you to do abundantly more than you can do on your own power. How liberating is that?!! You don't have to limit your Self-Care Action Plan to those things you know you can do. Why not remind yourself that you are a sacred woman who can do all things through Christ who gives you strength (Philippians 4:16) and just go after your heart's desire. Or, help someone else's dream become a reality. "The Black Girls Rock! Youth Enrichment Programs are designed to provide models of excellence and empowerment through dynamic mentorship." http://www.blackgirlsrockinc.com.
If there are girls in your life, you can start your own "Black Girls Rock" program and become a mentor. You will suddenly feel very powerful and brave when you are giving help and encouragement to the next generation.

Both of my sisters, Barbara and Ava, have started programs for girls. For several summers, Barbara, along with her granddaughter, Jessiyca, gathered young girls in the neighborhood and taught them to tap dance. She provided lunch and snacks; nourishment for the body. She also provided love and encouragement by helping the girls feel strong and powerful as they gained skill and built community; nourishment for the spirit and mind. Ava launched a lunch program during the summer at our family church. She provided not only food, but also activities and Bible lessons. Through their giving, both of them received more than they could have asked or imagined. Gain power by giving your talent, your time, and your love to others. You Got the Power.

D   DETERMINATION

And he said to them, "Suppose one of you has a friend, and you go to him at midnight and say to him, 'Friend, lend me three loaves of bread; for a friend of mine has arrived, and I have nothing to set before him.' And he answers from within, 'Do not bother me; the door has already been locked, and my children are with me in bed; I cannot get up and give you anything.

I tell you, even though he will not get up and give him anything because he is his friend, at least because of his persistence he will get up and give him whatever he needs. So I say to you, "Ask, and it will be given you; search, and you will find; knock, and the door will be opened for you." Luke 11:5-9

Jesus told this parable in Luke after teaching his disciples to pray the Lord's Prayer. He wanted to tell them a story that showed them in detail what it means to pray unceasingly; to keep praying until you get what you need and what you want. He taught them what it means to pray with determination. Jesus goes on to say that if your neighbor, friend, family member, or boss will eventually give you what you want because of your determination, then imagine how much more God will reward you when you ask, seek, and knock in faith. Never give up; God hears you. Give thanks that God always hears you. (Luke 11:41-42)

GOALS

By the end of this book, my hope is that you will:
- Recover, reclaim, and celebrate all that is sacred in your life.
- Begin to identify a renewed purpose for your life.
- Grow more curious about what keeps you healthy and do more of that.
- Take more time to listen to your inner voice--through meditation and prayer.
- Create a Self-Care Action Plan that is "all about you" that will become a self-care lifestyle.

- Believe you deserve the best. Seek your highest good in all you do.

You "are made in the image of God." That means because God is love and God created you. You can freely give love to yourself and others. Because God changes lives you, too, can change your life and the lives of others. You are created by God in God's own image. That makes you sacred and gives you the power to live a more healthy life of wellness.

I use a variety of ways to talk about what it means to be sacred and to live healthy and well, beginning with the importance of a relationship with God. When you develop, improve, or expand your relationship with God, your life will grow healthier in very basic and important ways:

- First, you will know that you deserve the benefits of God's creation—all good and perfect gifts come from God and God intends for you to have these gifts through the abundant life that comes from Jesus Christ. As you expand your relationship with God, you will be reminded that you are able to do more with less worry, less stress, and less anger, because you are living in God's strength, not your own. The things you do in the strength of Christ are done with joy and peace.

- Second, you will become more open to working toward a healthier lifestyle, because your body is a gift from God and is wonderfully made. It may have been difficult to pay attention to how you treated your body before, but now, you will be reminded that when you care for your body, you are honoring God. It may have been difficult to treat yourself as a precious gift before, but in each section of this book, you will be reminded that your body, just as it is, is a gift from God and you are valuable.

- Third, you will want to tell the story that you have discovered, recovered, and reclaimed healthy living for yourself. You won't be able to keep it to yourself that God has brought you health in a very spiritual and soul-changing way. You will want to pass on to your sisters, your daughter, your mother, the men in your life, to everyone the ways that God has changed your life. You will want to tell the story of a "new attitude;" you will want to tell the story of what health looks like for you. Old things have passed away and you will no longer look at your purpose in life in the same way. You will discover a new vision for yourself and for your future.

LIVE HEALTHY AND BE WELL
CORE PRINCIPLES

This book is about health and wellness, not simply about doing aerobic exercise to "get healthy," but creating a way of thinking about who you are that brings wellness and harmony into all parts of your life. Wellness is the sum of those ideals that bring you joy, that strengthen your relationships, that fulfill your dreams, and that lead you to a deeper connection to God: Joy, Love, Purpose, and Faith. These are the core principles of *Live Healthy and Be Well*.

In 2012, I wrote an article that was published in the *Journal of Religion and Health* called "Ethic of Resistance: Choosing Life in Health Messages for African-American Women." I explored how the media and public health agencies deliver news articles that build fear and lead to inaction because their messages are negative. Studies show that when African Americans hear negative health messages they are less likely to get health screenings than when they hear messages that empower and give hope.

In my article, I proposed that churches encourage women to tell each other more life-affirming stories that encourage them to become more healthy, to educate the next generation on what to do to stay healthy, and to create their own health messages that are grounded in Jesus' promise that we can have abundant life (John 10:10). When we hear life-affirming stories, we build a resistance to the negative images and messages that are so often a part of what we constantly hear about healthy living. "Black women get cancer less often, but die from it more than other racial/ethnic groups." "Black women have more heart disease, diabetes, HIV, etc." "Eat this or else you will get a disease or die." "Exercise this way or else."

Do these messages work for you? I absolutely am not motivated to get a screening if I can only expect to hear bad news. Or, at least, that is what the public health messages lead us to believe. We don't have to live with those messages. It is our opportunity as women of God to bring messages that call us into living with Joy, Love, Purpose, and Faith.

Joy, Love, Purpose, and **Faith** <u>are</u> the *Live Healthy and Be Well* Core Principles. These principles are the foundation for better health. These Principles are at the heart of every *Live Healthy and Be Well* story, every activity, and all of the meditations. When you live with joy, love, purpose, and faith, you are more willing to take action to be healthy and well. You will seek health information and put it into action: eat better, move more, learn what gives you joy, have faith in your wisdom and courage, and give yourselves the love you deserve. You will live with the vitality of having a sense of purpose that integrates all parts of your life.

My purpose is to improve the health outcomes of African-American women, to provide positive, inspirational health messages that are life-affirming, and to remind you that your faith must be followed by work. "For just as the body without the spirit is dead, so faith without works is also dead." James 2:26 It is action that leads to health and wellness as a lifestyle.

May the joy and love of God, the abundant life given to you by Jesus, the wisdom and strength of the Holy Spirit fill you and overtake your life.

DEFINING HOLISTIC HEALTH FOR YOURSELF

In our culture, we define "holistic living," "well-being," and "wholeness," as ways of integrating our minds, bodies, and spirits to have health and wellness in all areas of our lives. Everywhere you look in this pop culture

Live Healthy & Be Well - Hilda R. Davis

you hear these words and people telling you how to get there. This book is different. I may give you the activities, but you will tell your health story in your own way. Holistic health, well-being, wellness are all ways of talking about living with a spirit of joy, love, forgiveness, and peace, knowing God is present with you through it all.

I offer you mind-body-spirit activities to select according to what you want to achieve. Some of you will want to focus on physical health by using more of the "Body" activities. Others will want to try more of the "Spiritual" activities. You will have the opportunity to explore activities from all three areas: "Mind," "Body," and "Spirit" to create your "holistic" Self-Care Action Plan.

A holistic Self-Care Action Plan is the goal of your journey with *Live Healthy and Be Well*. This is more than an inspirational book with health activities. This is a journey where each chapter, each activity, every story draws you closer to the transformed life you desire. You deserve a renewed life of health and well-being, not just exercising more, not just eating more fruits and vegetables, but finding new ways to express joy, love, purpose, and faith in your life.

A holistic Self-Care Action Plan brings together all the parts that make you who you are: your emotions, your spiritual beliefs, and your physical strengths. A Self-Care Action Plan helps you to see areas you would like to change. You also will notice areas where you are satisfied with what you are doing. It is important to write down what you learn from the activities. In your supplies, you are asked to use a journal. The purpose of your journal is to track the changes you want to see and to celebrate what you are already doing. You will learn, in the final section of the book, how to organize your journal to complete your Self-Care Action Plan. Or you may use the blank pages in the Notes section at the end of the book to write your Self-Care Action Plan.

The journal is where you will record the thoughts from your activities, other things you want to add, or pictures that remind you of your self-care goals. Your journal is for you. It is your way of focusing on what you have thought about over the course of this book. It gives you a way of going back and repeating activities that were helpful. In your journal, you can challenge yourself to try something new.

Your journal will also be a way for you to tell others about your health journey. Whether you write in your journal everyday after you read the meditations, or once a week, or whether you find pictures to glue into your journal that illustrate what you want to say, it doesn't matter. It is your Live Healthy & Be Well Self-Care journal.

> Tools for the Journey: One standard spiral bound notebook or journal. Select a cover you are drawn to or spend time decorating the cover for your own pleasure. Colorful pen or pencil.

Each of the chapters builds upon what women like you have defined as being important for their well-being and health. The Bible story will connect to the theme of the week's meditation. These themes lead to greater teachings that are the basis for healthy living and a holistic lifestyle.

Each Chapter contains:

• An Opening with a suggestion for a guided meditation or prayer that will help you focus and relax into the moment.

• Bible stories of women who spoke boldly, took risks, and trusted God for the outcome.

• Personal stories that connect to the Bible story and makes the Biblical message come alive for daily living.

• A week of meditations to keep you inspired. The meditations use the strengths that form S.A.C.R.E.D.: Spirituality—Activates (Action)— Creativity— Renewal— Empowerment—Determination.

- Activities that connect to the Bible story and Chapter theme that ask you, in a fun and challenging way, to think in a new way about your body, mind and spirit health.

Remember, this is not simply a book that you pick up, read, and move on to the next thing. This book is a partner on your journey to a healthy lifestyle that integrates your body, mind, and spirit in a way that transforms and liberates you to walk a new path with courage. Return to this book and your journal over and over as you grow in the way God intends.

Take your time. Work through the exercises, read the stories, and use the meditations as daily reminders that you can *Live Healthy and Be Well*. You can invite other women to join you for a Bible study, use it as a book club selection, or you can read it in your sacred space at your own pace.

Live Healthy & Be Well - Hilda R. Davis

"TELL ME A STORY"

When my daughter was a child I read her a bedtime story every night. We had a daily ritual at bedtime. I would bathe her, turn off the telephone, and allow her to select her "favorite" book of the moment. Story time was our way of connecting with one another and to something bigger than both of us. Sometimes the stories were old folk tales, sometimes they were life histories of Black or African people, and sometimes the stories were just for fun but with a lesson carefully hidden in the rhymes and colorful characters.

However, the stories she loved most were the stories I told her about my childhood, about my life, about the dreams I have, about things I wish I had done differently. My story was the story she loved to hear over and over, funny stories of my sisters and brothers and me, stories about her father and me, and stories about the many twists and turns I've taken in my life. When my daughter heard my stories, she felt connected to me. I loved telling them because in some way I was giving her the gift of myself. Both of us gained something special.

> Stories—a way to build relationships and teach lessons that are pleasing to both the storyteller and the listener.

Look for these headings that point to the stories:
THE BIBLE STORY. . . is the main idea of the Chapter. I was led to these Bible stories because they have been life-giving to me. These stories are about Acsah, Shiprah and Puah, Hannah, the persistent widow, the woman whose son was healed by Elijah, and the daughters of Zeleophead. You may have heard of these women, but I wanted to tell their stories as examples of women speaking out and being seen. Their stories are about bravery and risk-taking in a society where women usually had no names, no voice, and no power. I have read and re-read them over the years and

have felt strengthened. Through their stories, you and I become part of their legacy of women who have taken risks, spoken their truth, and asked for what they wanted so they might live abundantly as God intends. TELLING OUR STORY. . . is taken from a personal experience, either my own or someone else's. The personal stories connect to the Bible stories. These stories are reminders that God's revelation continues to unfold in our lives today. Though our stories are centuries later, they show us how the power of God gives us the courage to live boldly, according to our truth

This book is a way for you to pass your story of health and wholeness to other women. You will be the storyteller who gives the message to others that there are choices that bring blessings and life and that there are choices that bring hardship and death. You will have the honor of passing the word to other women that will help them choose life as you choose life.

Jesus used stories to help the people following him to understand how to live an abundant life. In the Gospel of John 10:10, Jesus said that he came that we might have abundant life; a life filled with good health, with good relationships, with good choices. Jesus said that the thief comes to kill, steal, and destroy. We know many things in our lives that could destroy our health, steal our joy, and kill our bodies. We know that substance abuse (street drugs, alcohol, or prescription drugs, nicotine) can kill, steal, and destroy. We know that disease can kill, steal, and destroy. We listen to stories of people who died too soon from these thieves. We want to pay attention to the thieves of heart disease, cancer, diabetes, and hypertension. We could add to that list depression, loneliness, anger, and fear. All of these steal our joy and keep us separated from others.

> This book is to support you as you become a storyteller of healing—by telling your own story and the stories of others.

Live Healthy & Be Well - Hilda R. Davis

In *Live Healthy & Be Well* you will read stories that connect you to my life and to the lives of women in the Bible. Some of the stories will be stories of courage in the face of taking bold steps; other stories will tell of choices that did not bring the desired outcome, but brought transformation. But, isn't that how stories are? Stories bring us all the small and large details of life; stories connect to our hearts because they remind of us our own joys and pains; they remind us that others have felt as we feel; stories keep us connected to one another.

How do you tell other women—maybe your daughter or sister— stories of health and healing; stories of courage in spite of risks— to help them understand that some choices lead to life while others are not life-giving? You are the storyteller. I will share with you information and the encouragement that I hope will enrich your life. I hope that by the end of this book you will celebrate your strength and courage. I hope you will have an expanded story that includes new ways of living in health and wellness. Also, I pray you will be willing to share some of your story of hope and healing with others. But, most of all I pray you will receive Jesus' message of abundant life for yourself and then—tell the story.

God can dream a bigger dream for you than you
could ever dream for yourself. Success comes when you
surrender to that dream—and let it lead you to the next best place.

Oprah Winfrey (www.blackdoctor.com)

CHAPTER ONE: SPIRITUALITY

Opening

(You are invited to pray. You may use this prayer or one of your own):

O God, thank you because you made me as your precious creation. Thank you for this time with you to grow in health and wellness and love for you, myself, and others. In Jesus' name. Amen.

Or you may use this guided meditation: (Read this slowly, allowing time to feel the words. You may play soft music or light a candle to be the light of God.)

Meditation

Sit comfortably in your chair. Breathe deeply. Allow your body to relax. Picture yourself sitting in the sun. Feel the warm sun on your body. See the sun making the room bright with light. The love of God is the sun. Feel God's love as it warms your body. Let your body relax as the warm love of God touches you wherever you are tired, hurting, afraid. Begin to feel joy as your body becomes warmed by God's love. Relax for a moment and remember how much God loves you and how warm the love of God is. Remember how bright the love of God makes your life. As you slowly come back to the room, keep the light of the sun in your mind as a reminder of the love of God that lights your life.

Affirmation: (You may say this affirmation or create one of your own.)

I am created in the image of our loving God to give love and to receive love.

THE BIBLE STORY . . .

Joshua 15:16-19

Caleb said, "Whoever attacks Kiriath Sepher and takes it, I'll give my daughter Acsah to him as his wife." Othniel son of Kenaz, Caleb's brother, took it; so Caleb gave him his daughter Acsah as his wife. When she arrived she got him to ask for farmland from her father. As she dismounted from her donkey, Caleb asked her, "What would you like?" She said, "Give me a marriage gift. You've given me desert land; Now give me pools of water!" And he gave her the upper and the lower pools.

TELLING OUR STORY
The Spirit of God Gives Me Boldness

Have you ever been afraid, hesitant, or undecided about asking for what you want? I know I have missed out on big and little things because I did not want to say, "Yes, I want the diamond ring!" or "Yes, give me the raise because I deserve it." Sometimes, not asking for what I want has been because I felt I didn't deserve it. Other times, I didn't want to bring attention to myself; I'd rather the prize go to someone else. Probably, some of it comes from cultural messages that say, "Don't think too highly of yourself." These messages can be heard in church: "Be humble." "The first shall be last." "The meek shall inherit the earth." I grew up in the church and also heard these churchly messages at home. It is no small wonder that I am able to ask for anything at all.

Where was this Bible story about Acsah when I was a girl? I am captivated by a young woman living in a culture where women are viewed as property and have no voice other than what they are allowed to say within their realm (the household), who speaks up and asks for what she needs to take care of herself. She is given some dry land as a wedding gift, but when asked by her father what she wanted, she boldly asked for the best land with springs on it. In her culture, water meant life. She knew what she and her children needed to flourish. The Jewish Women's Bible

Live Healthy & Be Well - Hilda R. Davis

(http://jwa.org/encyclopedia/article/achsah-bible) interpretation said that she was getting a husband without property, which she a calls "desert land." Her purpose was to be able to provide a future for herself and her children by asking for land that was fertile and would be productive. She would not be dependent on what a husband without property could provide. She was not afraid to ask for what she wanted to live a prosperous life.

This is what I am thinking. ..

Think about the last time you asked for the best for yourself. Did you ask with boldness? Or were you willing to accept "dry land?" If you have been living in a dry space where you are not flourishing, then think about asking for something different. Connect to the power of God's Spirit in your life, which will help you speak, act and live boldly. You can take these steps to begin the journey to a more abundant, fertile way of living.

- To live spiritually is to identify what you need to live abundantly and ask for it.

- To live spiritually is to encourage beliefs that bring wellness to your life. Erin Grimes, my daughter, wrote an article for the Nashville Pride several years ago. It reads, in part. (The entire article can be found in the last Chapter of the book):

When I say I am going to heal, I mean I am going to discover the people and things that move me forward. Many times we look outside of ourselves to find the healing we need, when all along it was inside. In this process of self-discovery, I want to find healing. Everything I have been holding onto for the past twenty-two years that has not helped me move forward, I am letting go. This is a much needed gift that no one else could give me.

- To live spiritually is to have healthy relationships with others.

Live Healthy & Be Well - Hilda R. Davis

God created you to be in community with other people. Jesus built a community around him with his disciples. "Many women were also there [at the resurrection], looking on from a distance, they had followed Jesus from Galilee and had provided for him. Among them were Mary Magdalene, and Mary, the mother of James and Joseph, and the mother of the sons of Zebedee." (Matthew 27:55-56). The early church in Acts was a community of believers who shared all they had with one another. (Acts 2:42-47)

When you nurture a relationship with God, you ask boldly for what you want, practice choosing life and health in your decisions, and build a community of support.

SPIRIT* MIND* BODY ACTIVITIES

Take your time and use each activity as an opportunity to reflect on God's love for you and how you can honor God by loving yourself.

SPIRIT (The closer I get to God, the more I love myself as God's creation.)
Ask Boldly. Imagine you have a choice to make that is between what is good and what is best. What do you say to yourself that will allow you to speak up for your best? Is it a raise you know you deserve, but you have allowed yourself to sit quietly and just get by? Do you want more in a relationship? Have you been looking at those new shoes, but told yourself to "walk on by?" What should you do next to have what you want, not just what you need? You may write it down in your journal.

Let us therefore approach the throne of grace with boldness, so that we may receive mercy and find grace to help in time of need.
Hebrews 4:16

MIND (When I think about making a change, I have already taken action.)

Live Healthy & Be Well - Hilda R. Davis

Fun List. Make a list of fun things to do this week. Your list may look like this: Dance around the living room (with or without clothes). See a funny movie. Take a fantasy fun trip. Sing your favorite song. Laugh at yourself. Hug a friend. Go to the zoo. Reward yourself for reaching a goal. Get and give a back rub. Select as many from your list as you want and do them this week.

BODY (I take time to care for my body through prayer, self-care, or movement.)
Healthy List. Philippians 4:13 says, "I can do all things through Christ who strengthens me." Make a list of five healthy things you would like to try, but haven't had the time, the courage, the money, or whatever that may have stopped you. Select one from the list. Write Philippians 4:13 on an index card. Below that write, "I can do _____ (the action you want to do: become a vegetarian for a weekend, try a tofu burger, hire a personal trainer for a month, prepare to run a marathon, ask for what you want when making love) because Christ strengthens me." Post it where you can see it.

One More Thing

Identify one activity for your focus. Select an activity to write about in your journal. You may want to find a friend or family member to join you in the activity. Be aware of how having support strengthens your ability to just do it.

Closing

Close in prayer. Give gratitude for your successes and for what you have learned. Pray for the faith that God will give you the strength to ask for what you want with boldness.

S.A.C.R.E.D MEDITATIONS
Think on these things:
Spirituality Activates
Creativity*Renewal*Empowerment*Determination

Day One: Spirituality

"If I take the wings of the morning
and settle at the farthest limits of the sea,
even there your hand shall lead me,
and your right hand shall hold me fast." Psalm 139:9-10

Today think about this Psalm and the feeling of safety you can have when you trust God. If you go as high as the sky and as deep as the sea, God is there holding you "fast" or tight so you can know you are not alone. I have lived many places in my life. I started this roaming when I was in my twenties and moved from Detroit to Houston. I was not afraid, but I can only imagine how my mother must have felt. I believe I was not afraid because I knew even at that young age that God was in Houston, just as God is in Detroit. I am reminded of that as my own daughter has moved far away to attend college. She is held "fast" in God's hands: the left hand leads her and God's right hand is holding on tight to her. Today I am reminded that wherever I go, God is there and will never let go of me.

Day Two: Action

"If any of you is lacking in wisdom, ask God, who gives generously and ungrudgingly, and it will be given you." James 1:5

I don't know that it takes wisdom to act. I know in my own life I can see many times when even when the action was foolish, I didn't let that stop me from going full speed ahead. Thank God that things don't have to stay that way. Just because I made some foolish decisions before—once, twice, or maybe many times— today I can stop and ask God for wisdom before I act. God will not be mad at me because the other thousand times I didn't wait and pray and ask for wisdom. That is what it means by "ungrudgingly." God "ain't mad at me" for acting foolishly. I can get wisdom today if I just ask. Today is a new opportunity to receive God's wisdom, generously and ungrudgingly. I only have to ask.

Day Three: Creativity

"O Lord, you are my God; I will exalt you, I will praise your name, For you have done wonderful things." Isaiah 25:1

I have to praise God. My fingers are typing on this computer, my eyes can see, my mind is working. I have to thank and praise God that I have the ability to do wonderful things. I have a neighbor who is legally blind. He teaches others how to use computers. O Lord, I praise you for your wonderful works. I have a friend who lives with bipolar disorder. This is caused by a chemical imbalance in her brain. Her behavior will sometimes be "manic" and she finds it hard to relax. She does not want to sleep and is extremely happy and excited. Other times when she is in the "depressive" mood, she will be too tired to move. She will not leave the house and not allow anyone to come in. But, I praise God that with her medication, she takes care of her family, practices law, and leads workshops across the city. God, you have done wonderful things. Creativity takes many forms. You may not consider yourself creative, but God has given you the ability to do something wonderful; simply because you are God's creation. Blink your eyes, smile. Look at you! You are such a wonderful creation.

Day Four: Renewal

"I waited patiently for the Lord; he inclined to me and heard my cry."
Psalm 40:1

Sometimes, I am so tired that I am "too tired to spit." I get up early to read my Bible, go to work, run around at work searching for articles or sit and listen to my courageous, cancer patients, who inspire me though it is my job to bring them hope. Then, I run to teach a class. Finally, I can go home only to sit and grade papers until midnight. Then, I get to do it all over again.

However, this Psalm lets me know that if I wait patiently and let God know what I need to create balance in my life, God will hear my cry. But, first I have to pay attention to what my body is telling me. I have to know that it is time to pay attention to that cold that just won't go away. It is time to pay attention to my spirit telling me it is time for a change. I may have just gotten by before, but now is the time to sit and listen for the voice of the Lord. God is also listening for my voice. Today, when I cry out, God is there to listen. Today, when I realize enough is enough, God is there to listen.

Day Five: Empowerment

"Sing for joy, O heavens, and exult, O earth;
break forth, O mountains, into singing!
For the Lord has comforted his people,
and will have compassion on his suffering ones." Isaiah 49:13

I want to sing my song.

When I feel empowered, it is because I have spoken what is in my heart. I remember a sermon preached by a great preacher, Rev. Dr. James Forbes, Senior Minister Emeritus of Riverside Church in New York. I remember being moved by the message from his sermon titled, "Hannah Rose," but over the years the only phrase that has stuck with me is: "I want to be able to sing my song." He went on to say that it is a sad thing to die without having sung your song.

Though much younger then, I realized what a powerful thing it is to sing what is on your heart, to live what God has created you to live. That is what I got from that sermon. We must live the purpose that God has placed in us. We must encourage others if that is how we use our song. We must teach if that is our song. We can give and receive support and comfort; that is a reason for joy. Today, I will speak my mind so others will know what they can do to help. Or, when others need to be heard, I can offer compassion. I want to help others learn their songs, to hear their voices. Today, I will sing my song and not live in silence. God has given me a voice; I will sing my song.

Day Six: Determination

"Bear with one another and, if anyone has a complaint against another, forgive each other; just as the Lord has forgiven you, so you also must forgive."

Colossians 3:13

Forgiveness wouldn't be so bad if we didn't have to forgive people who were mean to us. If the only people we had to forgive were nice and kind, then it would be much easier to show forgiveness. Forgiveness takes determination. It is just not easy to overlook past hurts: physical, mental, and spiritual. I have forgiven before only to be reminded of my pain and become angry all over again. Then, I will remember the times I have not loved God with my whole heart and was given the gift of forgiveness. I am so grateful that God loves me just the way I am. Besides, God didn't ask that I forget only that I allow myself to heal, by forgiving. Today, I will find healing for myself by forgiving others.

CHAPTER TWO: ACTIVATE (TAKE ACTION)

Opening

(You are invited to pray. You may use this prayer or one of your own):

O God, thank you because you created me for action. You said you would never leave me or forsake me. When I move forward, I know you are going with me. Continue to strengthen me as I act to build a healthy lifestyle. In Jesus' name. Amen

Or you may use this guided meditation: (Read this slowly, allowing time to feel the words. You may play soft music or light a candle to be the light of God.)

Meditation

Sit comfortably in your chair. Breathe deeply. Allow your body to relax. Bring to your mind an action you want to take. As you continue to breathe deeply, bring to your mind this action. Repeat to yourself: "I am taking action." Begin to feel joy because you have taken this action. Feel your smile spreading from your face to your heart. Allow the joy of taking this action to spread all over your body. You are feeling joy. You are feeling proud of yourself. Know that you can feel this joy whenever you take action. You can feel this joy when you remind yourself, "I am taking action." See yourself taking this action. Feel the joy filling your body. Smile and feel proud of yourself. As you slowly return your attention to the room, repeat, "I am taking action."

Affirmation:
When I take action I can make changes, because the Spirit of God lives in me.

Remember to stretch yourself and add at least one activity to your Self-Care Action Plan at the end of each Chapter. Affirm and encourage positive steps to meeting goals. Congratulate yourself for taking action

THE BIBLE STORY . . .

1 Samuel 1-20

There was a certain man of Ramathaim, . . . whose name was Elkanah. . . . He had two wives; the name of the one was Hannah, and the name of the other Peninnah. Peninnah had children, but Hannah had no children.

Now this man used to go up year by year from his town to worship and to sacrifice to the LORD of hosts at Shiloh. . . . [Hannah's] rival used to provoke her severely, to irritate her, because the LORD had closed her womb. So it went on year by year; as often as she went up to the house of the LORD, [Peninnah] used to provoke her. Therefore Hannah wept and would not eat. . . .

. . . [But] Hannah rose and presented herself before the LORD. Now Eli the priest was sitting on the seat beside the door post of the temple of the LORD. She was deeply distressed and prayed to the LORD, and wept bitterly. . . .

As she continued praying before the LORD, Eli observed her mouth. Hannah was praying silently; only her lips moved, but her voice was not heard; therefore Eli thought she was drunk.So Eli said to her, "How long will you make a drunken spectacle of yourself? Put away your wine." But Hannah answered, "No, my Lord, I am a woman deeply troubled; I have drunk neither wine nor strong drink, but I have been pouring out my soul before the LORD. . . . Then Eli answered, "Go in peace; the God of Israel grant the petition you have made to him." . . .

Elkanah knew his wife Hannah, and the LORD remembered her. 20 In due time Hannah conceived and bore a son. She named him Samuel, for she said, "I have asked him of the LORD."

This is what I am thinking. ..

- Write in your journal what you and Hannah have in common that allowed you to take an action that led to your prayers being answered. Ex: Hannah went alone to the Temple to pray regardless of how it looked to the priest, Eli. She did not care what people thought; she took action in prayer in spite of having no evidence that things would change

Live Healthy & Be Well - Hilda R. Davis

TELLING OUR STORY
I Keep Going Until I Achieve My Goal

I was in high school when I first had the thought that I wanted to get a Ph.D. in psychology. I don't know where the idea came from because I did not know anyone with a Ph.D. I do remember liking my high school Psychology teacher. She was kind and paid attention to me. So, psychology seemed like a good thing to do. After graduation, I did go to college and graduated with a Bachelor's degree in Psychology. I did actually go on to graduate school to begin a Master's degree in psychology. I wasn't passionate about psychology, but I did really want a Ph.D. and thought I needed a Master's degree first.

But, life hit with a vengeance. I had to drop out of graduate school because of finances. I got a job, which I actually enjoyed, though it wasn't in psychology. Then, life just kept coming at me fast. I moved out of state to get away from the extreme cold in Detroit and an equally cold relationship. Many changes happened, but one constant remained. I wanted to earn my doctoral degree.

Fast forward thirty years, a call to the ministry, a wonderful baby—the marriage, not so much—but I graduated at the age of 51 with a doctorate degree in Religion and Psychology. It was not an easy journey. I had no idea it would take me so long or that so much would happen to delay my progress. But, my process continued. I continued to pray and hold the dream in my heart. I took action, doors opened. I thank God for answering my prayer and keeping the hope alive in me.

SPIRIT* MIND* BODY ACTIVITIES

SPIRIT (The closer I get to God, the more I love myself as God's creation.)

Overcome negative thinking. Hannah wanted a child, but year after year she was unable to conceive. However, she did not give up. Regardless of how long it took, Hannah overcame negative talk and despair while continuing to pray to God. God answered her prayer and she became a mother of a boy, Samuel. What helped you keep going in spite of challenges? How did you overcome negative thinking? Cut happy, positive words out of old magazines and paste on construction paper to remind you to focus on positive thoughts.

MIND (When I think about making a change, I have already taken action.)

You are a woman of action. Write a post card to yourself telling yourself what you want your "woman of action" to know. Example (fill in blank)

I am a woman of action. I like the courage I show when I

_____ _____.

I am a woman of action. I appreciate myself for

_____ _____.

I am a woman of action. I love the way I care for myself when I_____.

BODY (When I am active, my body feels better.)

Be Active. In order to take action, physical fitness is important for well-being. Yoga is one type of exercise that increases flexibility. "Yoga" is a Sanskrit word that means "yoke." When you practice yoga, you "yoke together" all parts of yourself: mind, body, and spirit. When you practice yoga, open your mind, pay attention to your breathing (your spirit), and relax your body. This is one yoga movement that will improve your flexibility if practiced

Live Healthy & Be Well - Hilda R. Davis

regularly. You may want to start your day with this:

- <u>stand</u> relaxed with both feet together; arms at your side
- <u>stretch</u> both arms above your head as comfortably as you are able (do not strain)
- <u>bring</u> both arms down to shoulder level and stretch them out (do not strain)
- <u>relax</u> both arms at your side
- <u>raise</u> one arm above your head; stretch upward; release arm to your side
- <u>raise</u> the second arm above your head; stretch upward; release arm.
- <u>repeat</u> these stretches whenever you feel yourself becoming tense.

Move to music. Put on a CD and move around the room to the music. Feel your body moving. Allow your mind to relax as your body moves, as it feels able. If you wish, remain seated, and move your arms, raise and lower your shoulders, move your head from side to side. Do not miss this opportunity to move your body and get the benefit of a fun activity.

One More Thing

Do you know how and who to ask for help when you want to take action? You may want to find a friend or family member to join you in an activity.

Closing

Write a prayer request in your journal. Record a prayer request that you have wanted for a long time. Keep praying while you align your will with God's will and take action.

S.A.C.R.E.D MEDITATIONS
Think on These things:
Spirituality Activates
Creativity*Renewal*Empowerment*Determination

Day One: Spirituality

For it is written, "You shall be holy, for I am holy."   1 Peter 1: 16

You are holy because you are in a relationship with God. Being holy doesn't mean that you have never done anything wrong or that you won't do unhealthy activities in the future. Being holy means that because you love God and are loved by God, you are whole. Being holy means you love God with your body, mind and spirit. Being holy encourages you to do the best you can for your body, your temple. Today, live holy because you already are.

Day Two: Action

Knowledge is 'potential power.' Only action produces results.
                                        ~ Jewel Diamond Taylor

To know what to do is a good thing. To go out and do what you know is much better. Trust your knowledge to lead you to the right action. Being a woman of action means that you are willing to act on your knowledge. Today, be guided by what you know and take action to do the right thing in your relationships and your health.

Day Three: Creativity

For we walk by faith, not be sight. 2 Corinthians 5:7.

There is a proverb that says, "When you come to the edge of the light you have been given and you are asked to take one more step, and all that might be there is a chasm, one of two things will happen. Either your foot will find firm ground, or you will learn to fly." This is faith. Faith is where you find your creativity. You do not have to know what is coming next. Use your creativity to step out on faith. Today, be creative and have faith in your ability to fly.

Day Four: Renewal

Peace, peace, to the far and the near, says the Lord: and I will heal them.
Isaiah 57:19.

Take a moment to sit quietly and think what it would mean to have peace in your life. Maybe it means that a relationship that is no longer working should be ended, now. You may have a special relationship that needs some attention, some kindness. You may have an opportunity to offer peace to someone who is hurting. Or, you may need to embrace the special relationship you have with yourself. Today, find what your temple needs to be a place of peace and healing. Find renewal and healing in your own temple.

Day Five: Empowerment

You have ideas, instinct, intuition, intelligence and imagination. Use them or lose them. — Jewel Diamond Taylor

Use it or lose it. Your power comes from using what you have. Allow your strong relationships to grow and help you become stronger. Be grateful for people in your life who believe in your ideas, intelligence, and imagination. Today, think of all the ways you have used your good ideas, instincts and intuition (gut feelings), intelligence and imagination. Write them in your journal. You got the power.

Day Six: Determination

Stay focused on your dreams and goals. Don't allow distractions, defeat, depressions, debt or dead-end relationships to keep you from growing.
— Jewel Diamond Taylor

Don't allow anything to stop you from becoming healthy. Don't let old boyfriends, new husbands, scared girlfriends, well-meaning family, out-of-touch pastors, or your own fears to stop you from your goal of health. Today, say no to one thing holding you back. Refer to your list of what it takes to be a woman of action. Be determined not to stop.

CHAPTER THREE: CREATIVITY

Opening

(You are invited to pray. You may use this prayer or one of your own):

O God, thank you because you made me to live creatively. I thank you for breathing creativity into me so I am a joint creator with you. Help me to glorify you in all I create. In Jesus' name. Amen

Or you may use this guided meditation: (Read this slowly, allowing time to feel the words. You may play soft music or light a candle to be the light of God.)

Meditation

Sit comfortably in your chair. Breathe deeply. Allow your body to relax. Bring your awareness to your body. Begin with your head. As you breathe, allow your face to relax. Notice any tightness in your head and neck. Breathe in the spirit of life, breathe out stress. Move your awareness down to your shoulders and chest. Relax as you notice any tension and allow it to release with your breaths. Continue to breathe out stress and follow your breathing from your abdomen, your pelvic area, and down your legs ending with the relaxing of your toes. Allow your body and mind to relax while you inhale the healing Spirit of God. End your body scan with one deep breath, knowing you can return to this peaceful feeling at any time. As you slowly return to the room, allow your deep breathing to be a reminder of the love of God that lights your life.

Affirmation:

I use my mind, body, and spirit to create and share joy, beauty, and love.

THE BIBLE STORY. . .

Exodus 1:15-21

The king of Egypt said to the Hebrew midwives, whose names were Shiphrah and Puah, "When you are helping the Hebrew women during childbirth on the delivery stool, if you see that the baby is a boy, kill him; but if it is a girl, let her live." The midwives, however, feared God and did not do what the king of Egypt had told them to do; they let the boys live. Then the king of Egypt summoned the midwives and asked them, "Why have you done this? Why have you let the boys live?"

The midwives answered Pharaoh, "Hebrew women are not like Egyptian women; they are vigorous and give birth before the midwives arrive."

So God was kind to the midwives and the people increased and became even more numerous. And because the midwives feared God, he gave them families of their own.

TELLING OUR STORY

Creativity Is Valuing Your True Self

Diane Palm is an artist; she is also one of my best friends. According to her, "For years I did not call myself an artist. I never put the label on things I did in the past. I just did things because I felt the need and pull to do them. Creativity soothes my soul. Now, I realize that I have been an artist all the time." Diane tells her own story and remembers her Aunt Fannie:

> I am a photographer and mixed media artist whose work has been exhibited at the Museum of Fine Arts, Houston, the Community Artists Collective, and other art spaces around Houston. I am an artist but my occupation is working as a manager in the juvenile justice system. Art is what occupies my heart, soul, and mind to the extent that I have pulled it into my job. I have increased opportunities for probation youth to recognize their strengths by integrating the arts into their programming. I believe that creativity

is not separate from life but is in all aspects of life. That's how Aunt Fannie lived.

Fannie was my mother's aunt and my great aunt, my grandfather's sister. Fannie was born in 1898 and Mom in 1921. Fannie helped raise Mom when Mom's mother died. So she actually "Grandmothered me." She moved to Pennsylvania during the Great Migration north in 1920s.

My Great Aunt Fannie showed creativity in recording her daily life in a series of journals from 1949, when I was a child, to the early 1970s. Aunt Fannie's daily life notes recorded the ordinary activities of her family and community.

I have Aunt Fannie's treasured journals now and draw inspiration from how she valued her life enough to speak about it. In doing this, Aunt Fannie, a minimally schooled, southern-born Black woman, made herself and women like her visible. She gave prominence to her life and women like her whose self-works go largely unnoticed and unappreciated.

Aunt Fannie also inspires me [Hilda]. What made a Black woman, living in Chester, Pennsylvania, who grew up during segregation and who was one generation removed from slavery, decide that the details of her life mattered? I believe that Aunt Fannie can answer that herself. Each day Aunt Fannie began her journal by thanking God. She might have said she was a God- fearing woman. The Israelite midwives were also described as "God-fearing." Having a connection to God allows us as women to know our value and speak or write what we know to be true. We find ways to be heard that make a difference to ourselves and others—sometimes to future generations.

This is what I am thinking. . .

- How does Diane's story connect with your personal story? Who do you say you are? Do you tell yourself who you are or do you let others define you in ways that might not suit you?

- Tell yourself who you are and live in your purpose. Write it down. Be willing to do what you believe you are called to do even when you are challenged. Be sure to take God with you.

SPIRIT* MIND* BODY* ACTIVITIES

SPIRIT (The closer I get to God, the more I love myself as God's creation.)

Write Your Life. Aunt Fannie wrote about her daily actions. Not a lot. But, she recorded the everyday moments of her life. She believed they were important and so that made them important. Here are excerpts from Aunt Fannie's journal

Did my laundry. [George] work half day. Diane here for weekend.

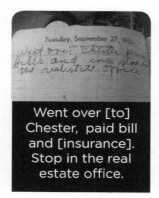

Went over [to] Chester, paid bill and [insurance]. Stop in the real estate office.

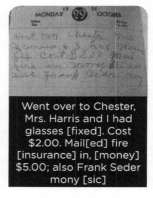

Went over to Chester, Mrs. Harris and I had glasses [fixed]. Cost $2.00. Mail[ed] fire [insurance] in, [money] $5.00; also Frank Seder mony [sic]

Record your own life for a week, or month, or continue— as Aunt Fannie did— for years. You don't have to write much. But, whatever you write is a reminder that your life matters; that what you say is important. Begin to value your own thoughts and words.

MIND (When I think about making a change, I have already taken action.)

Don't Worry. Be Happy. Laughter is a healthy way to reduce stress. Think of the last time you had a good laugh that caused you to "double up" with laughter. Install an app that sends you jokes daily. Play the Happy song by Pharrell Williams. Or, call a friend who makes you laugh and sip tea together. Take a break from bad, serious, and sad news—just one hour of happy. Take time during the week to remember the good feelings when things get too serious.

BODY (When I am active, my body feels better.)

> **Health is. . .** Write a definition of health that suits your lifestyle. The World Health Organization's definition of health is: "Health is a state of complete physical, mental, and social well-being and not merely the absence of disease or infirmity." Their definition is very broad. You will want to have your own definition of what health means to you. Your definition of health will include what is important to you. This definition will be your "health goal." Post your definition in a place where you can see it or add to your journal. Your definition of health may be: "Health means I pay attention to my 'gut' feelings; I learn to say 'no' when I don't want to do something; I will treat myself like a precious creation by eating vegetables _____ times a day, exercising _____ times a week, and listening to what my body pains and illnesses are telling me about my emotional well-being." Use this as a guide for creating your own definition of health.

One More Thing

It takes courage to write down your thoughts and feelings. It is not for everyone. However, just writing in your calendar is a record of how you spend your time and of what you value. Over time you will see what matters most to you or who. You will see an identity emerge. Is this who you thought you were? Or, do you need to begin thinking about bringing your body, mind, and spirit into harmony?

Closing

Pray to be reminded that each day you are writing the book of your life. Thank God for your story.

S.A.C.R.E.D MEDITATIONS
Think on these things:
Spirituality Activates
Creativity*Renewal*Empowerment*Determination

Day One: Spirituality

You have made known to me the path of life; you will fill me with joy in your presence, with eternal pleasures at your right hand. ~ Psalm 16:11 (NIV)

Sometimes it is hard to know what path to take. It can become difficult to choose among many choices that may seem worthwhile to do. But, if you just sit for a moment in silence, you can hear the voice of your spirit, the voice of God giving you the information you need. Paying attention to that voice that comes in the silence is God's way of reaching your spirit and giving you the wisdom that you need. Rejoice today that you can listen to your

> Try to find ways to move closer to doing the work that God created you to do.

own quiet, spiritual voice and know the path you are to take. When you listen to your spirit, you will take the path of life. Today be grateful for your wise choices that lead to a healthy life. Trust the voice of your spirit.

Day Two Action

Since, then, we have such a hope, we act with great boldness. . .
                                    ~ 2 Corinthians 3:12

The midwives, Shiprah and Puah, acted with great boldness, which took great courage. You, too, will have courage when you are acting because you are on a mission from God. Scripture said they feared God more than they feared Pharaoh—man. Think about what God has called you to do. You may need great courage and boldness to act, but your strength comes from God—not man.

Live Healthy & Be Well - Hilda R. Davis

Day Three Creativity

What you were born to do, you don't stop to think should I? Could I? Would I? I only think I will. And I shall. ~ Eva Jessye

You are a creative woman. You have the spirit of God in you. You were born to a particular purpose and you can know that purpose through watching what gives you joy. Listen to people who know you and are encouraging to you. Ask them what do they see that you do well. Think to the time when you were a child and what you loved to do. Remind yourself of times you have worked and not realized how much time had passed. What were you doing then? Begin today. Write one thing that gives you joy.

Day Four Renewal

He will yet fill your mouth with laughter, and your lips with shouts of joy.
~ Job 8:21

"Sit up. Sit up straight. Smile. Laugh. Laugh out loud." This is part of what this verse means when it says, "Fill your mouth with laughter." Look at yourself in the mirror when you laugh. Are you still mad? Still feeling depressed? No, this does not change the circumstances of your life. The bills still have to be paid. The work still has to be done. But, those things going on around you do not have to be the same as what is going on within you. You are your spirit, mind, and body. Feed your spirit with laughter and affirmations. Nourish your body with plenty of good water and fresh foods. Nurture your mind with good relationships. Sit up tall. Walk with good posture. Look like you are able to do all things through Christ and act like you believe that. Renew yourself each day with reminders of what you have been through and your courage. Laugh. Be renewed.

Day Five Empowerment

O Lord, my God, I cried out to You, and You healed me. ~ Psalm 30:3

There are days when getting out of bed is a reason for celebration because it is much easier to turn over and go back to sleep. Some days are just too hard to get through. The headache that threatens to take all your joy. The flow of blood that leaves you feeling weak and angry. The mean words spoken by the so-called friend. These are enough to make you cry out, "O, Lord, help me." The good news is that God does hear your cry. That does not mean the headache will automatically go away without the pain medication. (Don't suffer—pain medication can work miracles.) Nor does it mean that the "friend" will suddenly "get a clue" that when she says mean words that is not the same as telling the truth. However, when you give the stress to God, you can begin to hear the answer to your distress. You can relax. You can focus on solutions. You can make decisions from power not powerlessness. You can be healed when you accept the peace of God. Peacefulness brings healing. Find ways to have peace in your life today.

Day Six Determination

My daughter, Erin, at 18, decided that determination is one thing it takes to be a hero. She wrote,

> Webster's definition of a hero is a person of exceptional quality who wins admiration by noble deed especially deeds of courage. My definition of a hero is similar, but I have a few more criteria. Heroes do not have to be perfect, or someone who is known by all. A hero is someone who has <u>determination</u>, faith, and cares about people. . . . Having determination is not something that comes naturally. It means fighting until it pays off.

Think about ways you have fought until it paid off. Have you gotten a raise when you deserved it? Have you stayed in recovery when it would

Live Healthy & Be Well - Hilda R. Davis

have been much easier to go back to your life before you stopped using drugs? Have you left an abusive relationship for the last time when you had said you would leave many times before? Write in your journal what your determination has done for you. Congratulate yourself. <u>You are a hero.</u>

CHAPTER FOUR: RENEWAL

Prayer

(You are invited to pray. You may use this prayer or one of your own):

O God, thank you for renewing me today so I may rejoice in another chance to do your will. Thank you for your giving me the bold courage to grow in joy and love for you, myself, and others. In Jesus' name. Amen

Or you may use this guided meditation: (Read this slowly, allowing time to feel the words. You may play soft music or light a candle to be the light of God.)

Meditation

Sit comfortably in your chair. Breathe deeply. Allow your body to relax. Review a scene from your life that brings you joy. Who is in the picture? What are you doing? What feelings do you remember from this time of your life? Allow the feelings of safety, happiness, or love to fill you with joy. Sit for a few moments in these joyful feelings. Breathe deeply. Allow the joy to fill you with each new breath. Notice the slight smile on your face. This is what joy feels like. Tell yourself this is the joy that comes from allowing God to order your step and reorder your missteps.

Relax as you remember the joyful feelings. Enjoy being in a safe space that allows you to feel renewed. As you slowly come back to the room, keep the joy that abides in you as a reminder of the joy of God that lights your life. You can come back to this joy simply by breathing.

Affirmation:
Today I find hope for my future when I release the pain from my past and allow God to renew my soul.

THE BIBLE STORY . . .

2 Kings 8:1-6

Now Elisha had said to the woman whose son he had restored to life, "Go away with your family and stay for a while wherever you can, because the LORD has decreed a famine in the land that will last seven years." The woman proceeded to do as the man of God said. She and her family went away and stayed in the land of the Philistines seven years.

At the end of the seven years she came back from the land of the Philistines and went to appeal to the king for her house and land. The king was talking to Gehazi, the servant of the man of God, and had said, "Tell me about all the great things Elisha has done." Just as Gehazi was telling the king how Elisha had restored the dead to life, the woman whose son Elisha had brought back to life came to appeal to the king for her house and land.

Gehazi said, "This is the woman, my lord the king, and this is her son whom Elisha restored to life." The king asked the woman about it, and she told him.

Then he assigned an official to her case and said to him, "Give back everything that belonged to her, including all the income from her land from the day she left the country until now."

TELLING OUR STORY
People Can Restore~God Renews

. . . but those who hope in the LORD will renew their strength. They will soar on wings like eagles; they will run and not grow weary; they will walk and not be faint. Isaiah 40:31

What replaces a lost dream? Millions of people lost their homes between 2007 and 2011, which for many meant a dream was lost. I was one who lost a dream when my house was lost to foreclosure. I loved my house because it represented a dream of starting a wellness retreat center for women who wanted to spend a weekend or a week away from their daily responsibilities in peace and relaxation. One friend had named my place, Hilda's Haven. I hoped to obtain funding so the cost would not be out of reach for women living on a budget. Everyone needs a dream.

When the Shunammite woman walked away from her home and property for seven years, I believe she also walked away from some dreams for her life. Did she try to start over? How did she adjust her dreams? What made her keep going despite not only losing her property, but also being displaced to another country? I believe it was her faith that kept her going. I imagine she began to create a new life for herself, but she never lost sight of her dream. And because she did not lose faith, eventually, everything was restored to her.

This story resonates with me. My dream was restored, but revised. Rather than providing a physical space for a retreat, this book, *Live Healthy and Be Well*, offers women a spiritual wellness retreat~a virtual space of peace and relaxation. This space is not limited nor do you have to pack and prepare. If you have a *Live Healthy and Be Well* book, you can join me and other women in a community where you can experience joy and well-being without leaving your home.

Yes, property can be restored. Houses can be rebuilt, cars can be replaced, and you will even find another pair of favorite shoes. That is humanly possible. However, to bring renewal to your spirit and your dream—well, that takes faith in God. Trust that God will renew your strength, your wellbeing, and allow you to restore your dream. It may be bigger than before.

SPIRIT* MIND* BODY ACTIVITIES

SPIRIT (When I trust my spirit, I grow stronger.)

    Be still and listen. Your inner voice may be the voice of the Holy Spirit, giving you guidance on your health. Healthy religious beliefs are associated with:

        o higher self-esteem

        o lower blood pressure

        o higher overall well-being

Your inner voice can speak through Scripture. Your choice of scriptures can bring you well-being. In your journal, make a list of Scripture that have been helpful for you. Some examples:

    o "God is able to do more abundantly than we ask."
                    Ephesians 3:20

    o "If you have faith as small as a mustard seed, you can say to this mountain, 'Move from here to there' and it will move. Nothing will be impossible for you." Matthew 17:20

    o "For God did not give us a spirit of fear, but of love, power, and self-control."   2 Timothy 1:7

MIND (When I am aware of my choices, I grow in power.)

    Reduce anger. In Romans 12:2, the apostle Paul wrote, "Be transformed by the renewing of your minds. Think of ways you renew your mind after anger. Anger speeds up your heart, raises your blood pressure, and causes damage in your blood vessels—all lead to heart disease, the leading cause of death."

Some ways you can reduce anger are: Taking deep breaths; spending ten minutes a day for a week in meditation or centering prayer; being willing to go with the flow; admitting when you are

Live Healthy & Be Well - Hilda R. Davis

wrong and asking forgiveness; and trying a therapist. Write in your journal ways to renew your mind when difficult things happen.

BODY (When I am active, my body feels better.)

Love your body. List three things about your body that you complain about. List three things about your body that you appreciate. Now take those same three things and turn the complaint list into a list of compliments. Take the list of body complaints and tear it up. Treat yourself like a precious creation because you are. That includes your body. Post your list of six body compliments in a place where you can see them and appreciate your body. Renew your commitment every day to compliment yourself.

One More Thing

Renewal happens when you decide to change the story you tell yourself about your past. Try writing a different ending to a challenging story that shows how God was present even when it felt like you were alone. Imagine yourself renewed with a new story.

Closing

Pray that God will restore what has been lost and if your losses cannot be restored, pray that you can find renewal by adding a new ending to your story.

S.A.C.R.E.D MEDITATIONS
Think on these things:
Spirituality Activates
Creativity*Renewal*Empowerment*Determination

Day One: Spirituality

"Jesus said to the lame man, 'Do you want to be made whole?'" Luke 5:5-6

We have to want to be well in order to become well and whole. Play some soft music and sit in silence for five minutes. During that time, quiet your spirit and ask your spirit, your body, "What do you need to feel whole?" Wholeness brings together what you need for total health: mind, body, and spirit. Today, listen to what you need for your health and well-being.

Day Two: Action

"I can do all things through [Christ] who strengthens me." Philippians 4:13

We have to say no to risky behaviors. That is not an easy thing to do. Sometimes saying "no" may mean that we will lose relationships. Saying "no" may cause us to feel bad that we might have hurt someone's feelings. But, saying no to harmful actions, means that we are saying "yes" to the good life for ourselves. We don't have to practice saying "no" by ourselves; the love of God will give us strength. Today, say no to harmful behaviors and "yes" to the good life for yourself.

Day Three: Creativity

"Life has a natural flow, like a river. We experience frustration and problems when we try to fight the flow. Learn to go with the flow."
— Debrena Jackson Gandy

It is exciting to watch a National Geographic film on salmon swimming upstream. They leap, they hurl themselves forward, and they flop hard back into the water. They have to fight very hard because they are going against the flow. We root for them to win. They finally make it up the stream, but with only enough strength to reproduce. They are tired, worn out, and close to death. Don't live like a salmon—using all your energy toward an effort that leaves you empty. That is their destiny, not yours. You can go with the flow and save your energy. Today, don't swim upstream. Go with the flow, save your energy, and learn to relax.

Day Four: Renewal

"Come to me, all you that are weary and are carrying heavy burdens, and I [Jesus] will give you rest. Take my yoke upon you, and learn from me; for I am gentle and humble in heart, and you will find rest for your souls."
Matthew 11: 28-29

Rest, renew, be restored in the love of Jesus. You don't have to carry all your burdens yourself. In sickness—you are not alone. In grief—you are not alone. Jesus says that he will give you rest from all of your worries and burdens. Today, take time to make a list of your burdens. Write down things you cannot change on one page of your journal. Write "Jesus" on top of that page. You have just given your worries to Jesus. On the second page write down things you can change, but you may need help to start. Write "Community" on that page. When you feel overwhelmed with what you cannot change, look at the list with "Jesus" on the top and relax. Work on the list you can change with people who can help you.

Day Five: Empowerment

"For truly I tell you, if you have faith the size of a mustard seed, you will say to this mountain, 'Move from here to there,' and it will move; and nothing will be impossible for you." Matthew 17:20b

What are your mountains? Are there more bills than money? Do you have children who make you stay prayed up? Is your job a headache or such a joy that you work longer than you should? There are no mountains that are too large for just a little bit of faith. Your faith is your power. If you believe that things can change—then you can change them. Today, remember that, "little prayer, little power—much prayer, much power."

Day Six: Determination

"There is no fear in love, but perfect love casts out fear; for fear has to do with punishment, and whoever fears has not reached perfection in love." 1 John 4:18

When you have self-love you will have the determination to overcome many things. In Pearl Cleage's novel, *What Looks Like Crazy: on an ordinary day*, Ava, the main character, learned to overcome her fear of AIDS and her fear of dying through the love of her sister and a friend. Love is trustworthy and encouraging. Love is kind—not demanding. Love accepts you just the way you are. Today, allow the loved ones in your life to give you the determination to overcome fears. If you feel fear in a relationship, that is not love. Be determined to choose love, not fear.

CHAPTER FIVE: EMPOWERMENT

Prayer:

(You are invited to pray. You may use this prayer or one of your own):

O God, thank you for giving me the power and courage to make changes in my life. Remind me to turn to you, turn to others, and remember my inner strength when I face challenges. In Jesus' name. Amen
Read this guided meditation: (You may want to light a candle to be the light on your path.)

Meditation

I sit comfortably in my chair, breathe deeply, and allow my body to relax. I can feel the strength in my body, mind, and spirit. I am strong because I feel strong. I breathe in deeply and feel the strength of my breath. I am strong because I think strong. I breathe in deeply and know that God has given me a sound mind and power. I am strong because the Spirit of God in me gives me courage. I sit and breathe, relaxing as I remember the joy, the strength, the sound mind, and power I receive with every breath when I trust God for the outcome. I breathe. I relax. I am strong. I have power.

Affirmation:

I have the power to make a difference in my life and the lives of others.

THE BIBLE STORY . . .

Numbers 27:1-8

The daughters of Zelophehad, son of Hepher, the son of Gilead, the son of Makir, the son of Manasseh, belonged to the clans of Manasseh son of Joseph. The names of the daughters were Mahlah, Noah, Hoglah, Milcah and Tirzah. They approached the entrance to the Tent of Meeting and stood before Moses, Eleazar the priest, the leaders and the whole assembly, and said, "Our father died in the desert. He was not among Korah's followers, who banded together against the LORD, but he died for his own sin and left no sons. Why should our father's name disappear from his clan because he had no son? Give us property among our father's relatives." So Moses brought their case before the LORD and the LORD said to him, **"What Zelophehad's daughters are saying is right.** [emphasis mine] You must certainly give them property as an inheritance among their father's relatives and turn their father's inheritance over to them. "Say to the Israelites, 'If a man dies and leaves no son, turn his inheritance over to his daughter."

Empowered Sisters

The "sisters," Mahlah, Noah, Hoglah, Milcah and Tirzah, were bold and filled with the power of their common purpose. They were women in a culture where men ruled. They were orphans in a society where family lineage was destiny. They did not have money or land with which to barter. But, they did have faith. They had faith that God was on the side of justice, that God lifted up the oppressed, and that even the least mattered to God. It was this faith that—walking together—took them in front of the entire assembly, all men, to ask for what they believed they deserved: their inheritance. Also, they stood with each other. They did not stand alone.

These power-filled and courageous sisters were not asking for themselves only. They were asking for a stake in the "Promised Land" for their future generations. If they did not speak, their past would be lost and certainly their family would have no future. In spite of the obstacles that appeared to be against them, they had faith in what had been taught to them. They believed in their mission, they acted for the greater good, and they trusted God for the outcome. God gave them what they wanted for themselves and for their future. They preserved their family name, their well-being, and wealth for future generations. The sisters did not have a spirit of fear, but of love, power, and a sound mind. (2 Timothy 1:7) When you gather with others and speak collectively you have power.

TELLING OUR STORY
Pass It On

When our mother died, my siblings and I became the older generation. There are no parents, aunties, or uncles to be the keeper of the family traditions. We are it. So, in a sense, I understand what gave the daughters of Zelophehad their courage. If they did not speak for their family, if they did not think about keeping the family inheritance for next generations, then who would? There was no one else.

We had to make a decision to continue to honor family traditions. We are the keeper of family stories and it is our responsibility to pass them to our future. Our generation can make the difference in how our family legacy, our inheritance is remembered and maintained.

In the Jewish tradition they have *ethical wills*. An ethical will passes ethical values and how to live a moral life on to the next generation. How do you pass on your family values?

All of us have an inheritance. We have family memories, values, traditions, and a legacy we can pass from one generation to another and another. How do we maintain our family inheritance? It may require telling some family secrets. How many of us don't quite know how "Aunt Sarah" is related to the family? Or where the family jewels are really stored? Record these memories. Tell the stories. Get a safe deposit box, if necessary. Family legacies are fragile. If my sisters and remaining brother and I don't pass on our family traditions and legacy, they will die with us. We can't be afraid to speak the truth. Our future generations depend on us for their inheritance.

If you are part of the younger generation, step up and ask for your "inheritance." How will you know the family traditions unless you ask? All families have secrets that, as ours did, will die with the eldest member. Okay, you can't do anything about those. But, you can take your phone and record memories at the next family gathering. You can call aunties and uncles and ask them to tell you about their lives. My nieces and nephews, especially my daughter, will tell you I can't stop talking about what I know of the family. One day, you will be the older generation. I know, hard to think about. What will you leave for your children to remember about your life?

This is what I am thinking. . .
How does this story connect with your personal story? When have you spoken on behalf of those who could not speak or broken some rules and made a difference in the lives of others? What gave you your power to boldly stand for what you believe?

Thought Questions:
1.   It is a blessing to live the life of your dreams. If you are not living your dream life, this is an opportunity to think about what you want to change. What changes can you make now to write a different story? Make certain you are not avoiding change out of fear. Write your fears and then write how faith makes a difference.

2. Think about your parents, caregivers, and the people who influenced you as you grew up. How did they pass personal ethics, family values, and community traditions to you? What are some you remember? How can you create an ethical will for your family? Here is a resource for learning more about ethical wills. "Life Legacies: Preserving the Past for the Future" http://www.life-legacies.com/ethicalwills/

3. Who stands with you when it is time to take a bold step? Seek partners in faith who can support and encourage you even if they stand with you in spirit only.

4. For the next generations: Create your own history. YouTube, Instagram, or whatever the next generation of technology is, all give you the opportunity to leave an inheritance or to record your own history. You can do it with direction from God. After all, when you write the history, you have control of your own story!

SPIRIT* MIND* BODY ACTIVITIES

SPIRIT (God's spirit abides in me and gives me courage.)

Be Still. Centering prayer is one way to help calm your mind and pay attention to what is going on in your body. Centering prayer is sitting quietly and focusing on a sacred word. Practice centering prayer for 5-10 minutes. Sit quietly in a relaxed position. Close your eyes and think of a word (peace, Jesus, courage). When your mind begins thinking about other things, return to your word and repeat your word. Breathe deeply while centering. Allow the peace of God to fill your mind and body.

MIND (When I pray, my mind becomes aligned with God's will for my life.)

"Pray, unceasingly". Write in your journal a prayer that was answered, but you waited for a long time to see how the prayer was to be answered. Think about how God's answer was part of God's divine plan for your life. What recent goals have you set for yourself? Do you have health, career, family, or relationship goals? List your goals in your journal. What actions are you taking to reach your goals? Are your goals part of God's will for your life? Write pray unceasingly on a blank index card. Use your paints or colors to make it beautiful and joyful. Post where you can see it daily.

BODY (I am created in God's image and am divine.)

Take action. Take action. Take action. Sometimes that is easier said than done. Worry, stress, and illness can be a result of not being able to make a decision. Here is a guide to making decisions that may help move you off center and along the path to wellbeing. First, take a moment to be silent to pray and listen to what your spirit is saying. Second, write down your alternatives and what is good and bad about each of them. Third, ask others who have gone through a similar situation or whose advice you trust. Then, just do it. Trust God and make the decision.

One More Thing
Write down and practice those things that give you the power to speak boldly. Ex: Having a prayer with a friend, taking a small step every day for a specified period toward your goal, learning from the stories of others who were successful in a similar situation.

Closing
Pray for courage and strength to stay on the journey even when you cannot see the end.

S.A.C.R.E.D MEDITATIONS
Think on these things:
Spirituality Activates
Creativity*Renewal*Empowerment*Determination

Day One: Spirituality

For those who live according to the flesh set their minds on the things of the flesh, but those who live according to the Spirit set their minds on the thing of the Spirit. Romans 8:5

When you live from the "inside out," meaning making your spiritual health a priority, you are able to forget about age and live fully at any age. I have three "mother-friends" who are over 90 years old. Two of them are the mothers of my good friends. The third is a church member whom I adopted because I enjoy being with her.

They are all honest, kind, fun, truthful, and contemporary. One of them created a card when she turned 93 that listed her tips for longevity, *Guidelines to Embrace Longevity.* She is Mrs. Frances Jasper, mom of my friend Kay Hayes and her husband, Rev. Terrence Hayes, and grandmother to their daughters, Karolyn "Janee" and Francis "Cecilia." Pay close attention to what matters and the advice she gives to each of us regardless of our age. These tips will allow us to live well:

> "Life is an adventure. Embrace it. Have a thirst for learning. Share the Hope and Live the Joy.
>
> "Start today with praise and thanksgiving to God for another day. Be happy in the morning and keep going!"
>
> "Have a hobby and passion. Grow, nurture and develop."
> "Never lose your sense of humor!"
>
> "Healthy eating habits and exercise, along with self-esteem and

wisdom, are very important elements to a happy, wholesome lifestyle."

"Be at peace with God. With all of its shams and broken dreams, it is still a beautiful world. Be cheerful. Strive to be happy."
Mrs. Frances R. Jasper, Age 93, 2009.

I think my other "friend-mothers" would agree with Mrs. Jasper: Put God first, care about others, and enjoy your life. Now, begin writing your own Longevity Guidelines. Get excited about all the things you can do between now and 90!!

Day Two: Action

"But, I couldn't help it."

Have you ever said that about something you did that you knew was not healthy for you, but you did it anyway? "I just couldn't help it." You can. The next time you begin an action that you need to stop: 1) Think about the action 2) what you believe about the action 3) what are your feelings about what you are going to do 4) you can change how you respond. Example: 1) smoke a cigarette 2) "I should stop smoking." 3) "I get mad at myself when I keep smoking." 4) "I will go outside and walk, rather than take a smoke." Today, tell yourself that you "can help it." You can change your actions. Think about it.

Day Three: Creativity

"Dreams move you from where you are now to where you can be. Never stop dreaming."

What are your dreams? Don't say you don't have any. Think about when you were a child. What did you want to be? What made you happy? That little girl is there inside of you, wanting to see her dreams come true. Today, write down a dream from childhood. As a woman of wisdom, decide, "Is this a dream I can make come true today?" If it is, try it.

Day Four: Renewal

"Before healing others, heal thyself." Nigerian proverb

On a plane the flight attendant tells you to put on your oxygen mask first before you put on someone else's. You are not able to help anyone else if you are not well yourself. Today, find time to do special care for yourself. Don't put it off. You are the best person to take care of your needs.

Day Five: Empowerment

"I care for my body through prayer, relaxation, and movement."

After you do your exercise, take a few minutes to stop, rest, and meditate. Those five or 10 minutes of relaxation and quiet will give you energy to continue your day. Today, empower your body with physical movement and also empower your spirit with rest.

Day Six: Determination

"You have a dream that is waiting to live. Know that you have everything you need to live your dream. God's will for you is good."

What makes a dream "good?" How do you know that you are working toward something that is "good" for you? Think about whether it brings you joy and peace. Does thinking about your dream make you proud of what you can do? Does it feel like God's plan for your life? If you say "yes," then go for it. Be patient. Stick with it. Don't give it up. Today, make one small step that will move you closer to your dream.

CHAPTER SIX: DETERMINATION

Prayer

(You are invited to pray. You may use this prayer or one of your own):

O God, I thank you because you poured your strength into me. Thank you for the faith and determination to take bold steps in your service. In Jesus' name. Amen

Or you may use this guided meditation: (Read this slowly, allowing time to feel the words. You may play soft music or light a candle to be the light of God.)

Meditation

Sit comfortably in your chair. Breathe deeply. Allow your body to relax. See yourself walking down a path. The path is sunny and there are flowers on both sides of the path. You hear birds and the sun is just warm enough to be comfortable. You continue to walk. You look with wonder at the beautiful day; excited about what you expect to find on the path. As you walk, you realize you are ready for a refreshing drink of water, but you only see flowers along the path. You become a little anxious, but continue to walk because someone you trust has said there was a sparkling mineral spring on this path—exactly what you need to feel refreshed.

You keep going, but you notice you are becoming tired as well as thirsty. The flowers are not as pretty as they were when you started your journey, in fact, you hardly notice them. The sun feels a little warmer than before. You keep walking; not because you know what is ahead, but because someone you trust told you a cool, refreshing stream of water was ahead of you on the journey.

You are beginning to slow down. You think about turning around and going off the path and exploring on your own. You begin to think you can find your own way. Maybe, the person you trust does not know where the stream is. Maybe, you are on your own and should give up. But, because you are not sure what else to do, you keep going.

Just as you begin to doubt this path, you hear what sounds like water. The sound is faint at first, but you begin to walk faster on the path and it is water you hear. You begin to run and now you can see a beautiful stream with abundant flowers and tall green plants. There is a beautiful crystal pitcher for dipping into the clear sparkling water. You also notice a water glass in your favorite color sitting with the pitcher on a big tray. Also, your favorite fruit sits in a bowl on the tray.

You are so happy that you did not give up. Your determination has paid off. You have more than you could have asked or imagined. You are grateful for trusting. This is a resting place. Your journey will continue after you are refreshed. Rest. Breathe. Continue to believe that God directs your path and only wants you to have a good life. Just trust, have faith, believe, and never give up.

Affirmation:
I stay on my path with the faith, courage, and determination to step into God's purpose for my life.

THE BIBLE STORY . . .

Luke 18:1-8a

Then Jesus told his disciples a parable to show them that they should always pray and not give up. He said: "In a certain town there was a judge who neither feared God nor cared what people thought. And there was a widow in that town who kept coming to him with the plea, Grant me justice against my adversary.'

"For some time he refused. But finally he said to himself, 'Even though I don't fear God or care what people think, yet because this widow keeps bothering me, I will see that she gets justice, so that she won't eventually come and attack me!'"

And the Lord said, "Listen to what the unjust judge says. And will not God bring about justice for his chosen ones, who cry out to him day and night? Will he keep putting them off? I tell you, he will see that they get justice, and quickly. "

TELLING OUR STORY
Prayer Gives Determination to Keep Going

What did this widow want that made her so persistent—so determined? Maybe, she needed money that was owed to her. She may have wanted to start a business like Lydia, who in Acts 16:14 sold purple cloth, or have her property restored like the widow we met in 2 Kings 8:1-6 (Bible story in Chapter Four, Renewal). Her low social standing as a widow meant she did not have the power to demand anything. She did not have the money to buy the judge. She did not have power or money, but she had persistence.

As a coach/counselor, I work with women of all ages. My clients range in age from teenagers on the brink of womanhood to women who are retired. There are many things they have in common. All of them want joy, good relationships, and meaning in their lives. One of the questions I often hear is, "What should I be doing with my life?" Or, they ask, "How do I reach my dream?" Regardless of their age, it is important that we spend the time to identify the career, ministry, or lifestyle—the dream—that will give their lives meaning. Then we work to figure out how to make their dream—their career, ministry, or lifestyle—happen.

One book I have used that I love gives tools and a workbook for finding what your next career step should be. Pamela Mitchell wrote _The 10 Laws of Career Re-Invention: Essential Survival Skills for Any Economy_, which is an excellent read if you want to uncover your career passion; then use her road map for changing careers. I think two of her laws are also useful if you want to understand your purpose or find more meaning in other parts of your life. Mitchell writes in Law 1: "Have a Vision for your Life" and in Law 9: "It Takes as Long as It Takes."

How do you identify your vision— a vision you are passionate about? How do you know that what you are doing is your best life? Go to God in prayer.

You may have a vision, like the widow did. She was going back to the judge for something that was important to her. So, you want to know how to make your vision a reality. Keep praying. You pray, "God, show me your plan for my life. Help me to clearly know what I am to do now." And you keep going back; you continue to pray. You wonder, "When will I know what is right for me?" You pray more.

As you pray, you become clearer on what you want. You learn to listen to God and pay attention to the small voice that gives you the path to take. You pray not to change God's mind, but to gain more clarity about your purpose. You also learn patience.

Mitchell's Law 9 says that getting to your new thing or next

Live Healthy & Be Well - Hilda R. Davis

opportunity "takes as long as it takes." Or as the Gospel song says, "It may not come when you want it, but it's always right on time." Each time you approach God in prayer you grow in faith that God will supply the answer that will give you the best outcome. You may want your answer by your birthday, in time for Christmas, or before you walk down the aisle with Mr. Right Now! God's answer "takes as long as it takes." You are not just "re-inventing your career" you are creating a new life. Have faith that your best answer will come. Be determined. Keep praying.

This is what I am thinking. . .

- What makes you keep going when you feel like giving up?

- Who helps and supports you when you need encouragement? How can you help and support someone else?

- Write a prayer for yourself you can pray when you feel like stopping or when you need encouragement. God hears you.

SPIRIT* MIND* BODY ACTIVITIES

SPIRIT (My joy comes when I listen to my spirit.)

> **Healing your past.** Ask a friend or family member to support you while you do this. Write an unpleasant memory or memories. As you write them say, "God, I give you this memory. I release the pain to you." (If unpleasant memories become too difficult, please stop.) Create a prayer or meditation to be used to bring healing to those memories you regret. Say, "God, today I choose your blessings. Fill me with the fruits of your Spirit: love, joy, peace, patience, kindness, generosity, faithfulness, gentleness, and self-control (Galatians 5: 22-23) Release painful memories and make room for new joyous memories.

MIND (When I focus on my goals, I am more confident of my path.)

Passing it on. Think about a time that you have brought encouragement to a friend, relative, or maybe a stranger. How did you do that? Tell that story. Make an opportunity to allow God to use you this week. Help someone else do something that is hard for them. Go with them, send them a note of encouragement, or give them a call.

Celebrate yourself. If you are living your dream, working towards your dream, or trying to identify your dream you are invited to a celebration for you. Use construction paper and decorations to make yourself a celebration card! You are celebrating yourself. You deserve it!!

BODY (When my spirit and mind are in harmony, my body feels well.)
Breathe and stretch. Stand. Take two deep full breaths. Allow your stomach to expand as you breathe in and relax as you breathe out. Next, allow your head to fall gently forward, then roll it around to the right, back, to the left, and then return it to gently rest it on your chest. Do this two times. Raise your head to look straight ahead. Gently raise your right arm (as you are able); release it back down to your side. Gently raise your left arm (as you are able); release. Now raise both arms and stretch them as high above your head as you are able. Relax both arms. Do this stretch each day and whenever you feel stressed.

(If your mobility is limited, sit quietly and listen to your breathing. Pay attention to the sounds you hear in the background. Let go of the stress in your body by naming each part of your body and saying, "Eyes—let go of stress." "Neck—let go of stress." "Shoulders—let go of stress." Name parts of your body from your head to your feet. Then repeat, "I live in healing peace and I am grateful for my relaxed body.")

Live Healthy & Be Well - Hilda R. Davis

One More Thing

What does your path look like now? How do you stay on your journey even when there are no flowers and when you are tired? What about your faith keeps you from giving up? Pick one activity for this week's focus. Select an activity to write about in your journal.

Closing

Pray that when you have to "stand" that God will send support to stand with you.

S.A.C.R.E.D MEDITATIONS
Think on these things:
Spirituality Activates
Creativity*Renewal*Empowerment*Determination

Day One: Spirituality

"Sometimes all it takes to be a blessing to someone is a kind word."

Today I called a friend I had not talked to in almost 10 years. She was so happy to hear from me. She said, "Your call has made my day." Think about the times you have gotten a call from someone that made your day. Today give a kind word or make a quick phone call. These are small actions that can make you and the receiver happy.

Day Two: Action

Here are three steps to achieving your dream:

1. Define your dream.
Use action, specific words: "I see myself preaching to 1,000 people beginning next month and being compensated well."

2. Start working toward your dream today.
What can you do today to begin working toward your goal? Do you need to begin speaking to small groups in your church? Do you need to take speaking classes? How do you need to market yourself? What small steps can you begin today?

3. Measure your progress.
Evaluate your progress after one week, two weeks. Have you spoken before any groups? Have people invited you to speak? Do you need to tell more people, take bolder steps, pray and be led by

the answers? Or, assess your dream. Maybe, there is a dream right in front of you that you haven't noticed. It does not have to be hard to live your dream life.

Discuss with a friend how she can support you as you accomplish your dream. Ask how you can be a support. Believe you can achieve your dream. Show gratitude by helping her reach her dream.

Day Three: Creativity

"Affirm the many ways you are creative."

How often have you said, "I am not creative" when you see a beautiful painting or hear a great song? Well, don't say that anymore. Think about the things you can do. Are you a great cook? Do you work with people well? Can you keep a baby happy? Who styled your hair? Are you complimented on how stylish your clothing choices are? You are creative. Today, just claim your blessing by acting on your creative thoughts. Write them and celebrate yourself.

Day Four: Renewal

"Be grateful. Take the time to say thanks to those who make your life happy."

It is always easy to complain and moan and whine. Sure, things are not what they could be, but as they always say, they could be worse. Tell someone you are grateful for what they have done for you. Give someone a hug of thank you for their thoughtfulness. Give yourself a pat on the back for helping someone. Today, be renewed by being thankful.

Day Five: Empowerment

"It is harder to break a bundle of sticks than just one stick by itself."

You are stronger when you don't try to do everything by yourself. Don't be too ashamed, too proud, too scared, too angry to ask others for help. Just as you help others; when you allow others to help you, you grow stronger and so do they. Today, don't try to do hard things by yourself. Get help and get powerful.

Day Six: Determination

"Ain't gon let nobody turn me around."

This song tells us not to let "nobody" turn us around. Sometimes things can turn us around. Sometimes we turn ourselves around when we are afraid to reach "higher ground." Today, speak determination into your spirit and don't let "nobody" stop you from being a blessing to yourself and others. Don't let your own negative thinking hold you back. Keep Going.

THE CLOSING

Now what I am commanding you today is not too difficult for you or beyond your reach. It is not up in heaven, so that you have to ask, "Who will ascend into heaven to get it and proclaim it to us so we may obey it?" Nor is it beyond the sea, so that you have to ask, "Who will cross the sea to get it and proclaim it to us so we may obey it?" No, the word is very near you; it is in your mouth and in your heart so you may obey it." Deuteronomy 30:11-14

This passage from Deuteronomy 30 is in the middle of Moses' farewell speech to the people of Israel. They had been released from bondage in Egypt, survived the wilderness journey, and were now very close to reaching their goal that God had promised to their ancestors. This was a time of high spirits and optimism, for all except Moses. Moses was not entering the new land and a new life with them. However, he loved his people and had words for them to encourage and inspire them.

These words are part of a Chapter of wise advice and blessing. Moses knew what they were facing and wanted to prepare them and remind them of who they were and what they had already done by the strength of God. He tells them this task of starting a new life is not too hard for them. In fact, they have everything they need within them—in their speech and in their spirit.

This passage is a reminder that your next step to achieving your wellness goals is not too hard for you or out of your reach. You don't have to wait for someone to make it happen for you. If your goal is to eat healthier, you can do that. If you want to change careers, that is within your reach, too. If you want better relationships or a new relationship, the Spirit of God within your heart gives you the strength, the courage, and the wisdom to cross from the old place into the promise of the new. God is present. The Spirit of God is as close as your breath.

Moses also says in Chapter 30 that it is up to the people of Israel to choose—today: life and prosperity or death and destruction. You also choose everyday: healthy choices or choices that keep you stuck; the opportunity to step out in faith or to remain in the same place because of fear. You can do it. The Spirit of God is in you!!

TELLING MY STORY
Choosing Life

Written by my daughter, Erin Grimes, at age 21

The summer I graduated from Dillard University in New Orleans, Louisiana, was a tumultuous and life-altering year due to Hurricane Katrina. Graduation was the ultimate triumph for me and my classmates. Against all odds, 354 students received their degrees on July 1, 2006. It was an occasion to be proud of ourselves and to give thanks to God.

Before the hurricane hit, I had big plans for after graduation. I was headed for New York for graduate school. My senior year could not go by fast enough. I was ready to reinvent myself and be completely on my own. Going from one big city to another big city, and not having to go back home to live, was my idea of success.

Once the levees broke after Katrina and Rita, my plans were drastically altered. My focus was readjusted from planning for the months ahead to just trying to get through each day. This strategy got me back to Dillard after a semester away. However, I was unable to think about graduate school at all, which sent me on a hunt for a graduate school that had later application deadlines at the last minute. I looked everywhere and decided on the University of New Orleans (UNO), but God had a different plan for me.

I received admission to UNO, but housing and financial aid did not come as easily. I was trying to force my old ideal life into my new post-Katrina one. It did not work. The reason for my trying to maintain this ideal life was so I would not look like a failure in the eyes of my family and my community. Yet, I did not realize the only person who was placing this ideal on my life was me. To my family, getting my degree was a feat in and of itself, which made everything else the icing on the cake.

After months of stress and worrying about graduate school, I have returned home. I no longer see being at home as a failure, but as some much needed "me" time. I can begin my healing process. India.Arie has a song on her second album titled "Slow Down." Even though she wrote this song long before my dilemma, it feels like she is speaking to me. In the chorus, she states, "Slow down baby ya goin' too fast. You got your hands in the air with your feet on the gas. You 'bout to wreck your future, running from your past. You need to slow down before you go down baby." I was truly about to make a mistake, trying to make up for what I could not do after Katrina.

There is so much value and power in being able to take care of yourself. By continuing to ignore the great affect Katrina had on my life, I was not doing my spiritual health a favor. We cannot overlook our frame of mind and mental stability in order to achieve a goal. There is no failure, or disappointment, in slowing down. We all should continuously take our mental and spiritual health into account. Not taking them into account can damage you in the long run more than slowing down ever could.

Please, never hesitate to slow down and have some personal time. Bad spiritual and mental health is not only detrimental to you, but your family as well. Whether you go on a trip, get a massage, or simply stay in the bathtub a little longer, slowing down is necessary. I pray that all of you will take my story and know there is not failure in taking a moment to clear your head and heal.

Live Healthy & Be Well - Hilda R. Davis

GO IN PEACE

You have come to the end of this book, but not the end of your journey to health and wellness. You are defining your own way of thinking about what it means to be healthy. You may already have known a lot. You may already eat right and exercise and think good thoughts. But, each day is starting all over again, making a new commitment to your health.

Start with Appendices 1 and 2 where you will find tools for building your Self-Care Action Plan. These tools allow you to select those areas you wish to improve and even add some new actions to what you are already doing.

Your spirituality is always there to help you start each day fresh and new; being grateful for what you did well and learning from your challenges.

To live spiritually is to live being aware of how much God loves you. Once you accept God's love for you, it is easier to love others. The way to love others is to love God and love yourself. Your mental and physical health balance each other; what they balance on is your spiritual health. When you have a strong connection to God, then the foundation for your physical and mental health is strong enough to support you through a crisis.

I offer you three ways to think about your spirituality, which is the power of God's love in your life:

1.   To live spiritually is to invite into your life the healing power of God's love. Everyone has memories that are painful and may bring shame and guilt. You can become free by remembering that God loves you unconditionally. Spirituality or spiritual growth

comes when you are able to feel God's love through a personal relationship with God. A personal relationship with God comes through prayer, silence, reading Scripture, and being available to the mystery of God's unconditional love.

2.   To live spiritually is to encourage beliefs that make sense for who you are today rather than past beliefs that may keep you tied to guilt and shame. Julia Boyd, in her book, <u>Girlfriend to Girlfriend: Everyday Wisdom and Affirmations from the Sister Circle,</u> says,

> Shame and guilt can't stand up to solid reasoning because it wears them out. Shame and guilt are thoughts that are generally connected to the past in some way. We think about what we "should have," "could have," or "would have" done differently, but there's no way to recapture the past so when we have those thoughts in the present, we get caught in the tangled web of shame and guilt, which is more harmful than helpful. (p. 45)

A healthy spirituality allows you to turn to God's love for forgiveness, rather than past beliefs that do not encourage healing and forgiveness.

3.   To live spiritually is to have healthy relationships with others. God created you to be in community with other people. Jesus built a community of women around him along with his disciples. "Soon afterward he went on through cities and villages, preaching and bringing the good news of the kingdom of God. And the twelve were with him, and also some women who had been healed of evil spirits and infirmities: Mary, called Magdalene, from whom seven demons had gone out, and Joanna, the wife of Chuza, Herod's steward, and Susanna, and many others, who provided for them out of their means." Luke 8:1-3

You grow spiritually when you nurture a relationship with God, practice letting go of shame and guilt and learn to forgive yourself and others. The women who followed Jesus were not perfect; they were forgiven. Forgiveness and love bring healing.

Find, build, and support loving relationships.
Celebrate your courage and determination to make changes.
Take your new path to health and wellness.

GO WITH GOD TO LIVE IN JOY, FAITH, PURPOSE, AND LOVE.

Appendix 1

Your responses to this Affirmation Sheet will help you customize the most motivating, energizing, and holistic Self-Care Action Plan for your optimal health. Don't limit yourself to what is listed here. Add to your plan what works for you.

HEALTH STAR

YOU ARE A STAR

Read the All-Star Affirmation sheet on the next page. Identify actions that are part of your current health practices. Add a star to those blocks because you are a star at this activity. Place stars in all the boxes that describe what you do to care for your body, mind, and spirit. This sheet shows you the actions you already do.

> 1) Use it to create your own positive messages that affirm that you are living healthy.

> 2) Make a copy of this All-Star Affirmation sheet and hang it as a poster that shows how well you take care of yourself.

Live Healthy and Be Well! Celebrate Yourself!

If you do not do an activity and did not put a star in a box, add that action as a goal for your Self-Care Action Plan to work on later. These actions will give you goals for your next steps as you improve and bump up your wellness plan. Either way you are a winner because you are starring in your own health!!

ALL-STAR AFFIRMATIONS

I usually sleep 7-8 hours a night	I can touch my toes (even if I must bend my knees!!).	I drink 6-8 glasses of water a day.	I can laugh at myself.
I eat at least one leafy, deep green, or orange vegetable every day.	I eat at least one piece of fruit every day.	I have at least one good friend.	I do not smoke.
I have positive spiritual beliefs.	I pray or meditate 3-4 times a week.	I enjoy doing something for myself once a week.	I take time for myself everyday.
I exercise 3-4 times a week.	I never drink and drive.	I treat myself like a precious object by taking time to relax— even 20 minutes— daily.	I have had a mammogram or a health physical this year.
I love the work I do	I gain satisfaction by volunteering.	My relationships are satisfying.	I believe I can achieve my health goals.

Appendix 2

Answer the questions in this Self-Care Quiz. If you answer "OK" or "Need Strengthening" add those items to your Self-Care Action Plan as one of your Body, Mind, or Spirit goals.

SELF-CARE QUIZ

Part I: Instructions: In front of each item put one of three initials:
E = I am excellent in this.
OK = I am acceptable, but I have room for improvement.
NS = I need strengthening here.

_____ 1.   I listen to my body and learn from what it's trying to tell me (like "Slow down and play a little!").

_____ 2.   I enjoy spending some time each day, giving my body loving self-care to increase its aliveness, it attractiveness (especially to myself), and its power.

_____ 3.   I am learning to resolve my so-called negative feelings, such as guilt, shame, jealousy, unforgiveness, anger, resentment, loneliness, despair, fear, so that they don't keep me from my God-given happiness.

_____ 4.   I practice the fine art of forgiving myself, thus becoming better able to forgive others and life. I know that God has forgiven me first.

_____ 5.   I give my mind-body-spirit the daily gift of a quiet time such as deep relaxation, meditation, inspirational reading, or prayer to reduce stress and recharge my batteries.

1. I plan to increase my exercise by:
     a) Walking to the corner and back
     b) Taking the stairs instead of the elevator
     c) Becoming more flexible by bending to the floor and stretching up toward the ceiling
     d) Training for a marathon
     e) Taking a dance or aerobics class

2. I plan to change my eating habits by:
     a) Eating more vegetables and fruits
     b) Trying one vegetarian meal a week
     c) Drinking tea, water, or juice instead of soda
     d) Drinking two to four glasses of water every day
     e) Eating red meat only once a week and replacing meat with fish or poultry

3. I plan to increase the time I spend:
     a) Praying or meditating in silence for 10 minutes
     b) Writing in my journal for 20 minutes
     c) Reading inspirational quotes or articles
     d) Reading the Bible
     e) Listening to quiet music instead of the news

4. I plan to improve my emotional well-being by:
     a) Turning off the television and going outside
     b) Avoiding negative messages and negative people
     c) Reading my affirmations
     d) Bringing a smile to someone's life
     e) Giving a gift to someone who cannot repay the kindness

5. I plan to educate myself on my health by:
     a) Getting a physical exam or a scheduled screening and learning what the test results mean
     b) Learning the symptoms of diabetes, heart disease, and stroke
     c) Listening to my body when it is tired–sad– mad– happy–hurting and taking action to change
     d) Telling others what I learn about how to live healthy and be well
     e) Learning about drug interactions and asking for alternatives if my medications have too many side-effects

Add to your Self-Care Action Plan all the areas that you selected from the Self-Care Quiz, parts 1 and 2." Use the results from your Quiz, your Mind*Body*Spirit Activities found in each Chapter, and your All-Star Sheet for your Self-Care Action Plan. Also, add any areas you wish to improve.

If you feel you don't have time for one more thing and that "thing" is your health, then you really need to create a Self-Care Action Plan. This does not mean changing your entire life in one day. It means that you notice when you are stressed, in pain, unhappy, anxious—then take action.

Appendix 3

YOUR SELF-CARE ACTION PLAN

Turn to a blank page in your journal or in the Notes section starting at page 97. Write at the top of the page in big letters: "SELF-CARE ACTION PLAN." Now divide the page into three sections: Mind–Body–Spirit and under each heading write one (1) Goal that you want to improve. You may want to work on more than one but begin with one at a time.

Under your Goal, write How you intend to accomplish your Goal. Next, write Who you will get to help you with that Goal. Finally, write When you expect to start. Your page should look something like the following Chart. You can make it as detailed or as simple as you like. Or use the template, Appendix 4, for your Self-Care Action Plan.

MIND	BODY	SPIRIT
GOAL: Repeat daily affirmations.	GOAL: Eat fresh produce.	GOAL: Read one verse from book of Psalms daily.
HOW: Use affirmations from SACRED Women.	HOW: Buy pre-washed vegetables/salads.	HOW: Add reminder to calendar or on phone.
WHO: Have friend repeat with me by telephone.	WHEN: Eat at least one serving daily.	WHO: Ask prayer partner or friend to join in reading Psalms.
WHEN: Begin today.	GOAL: Plan an easy exercise —	WHEN: Read 6 AM every day or before my day gets busy.
	HOW: Park at far end of parking lot	
	WHO: Ask co-worker to remind me.	
	WHEN: Do three times a week begin Monday.	

Live Healthy & Be Well - Hilda R. Davis

Appendix 4

MIND	BODY	SPIRIT
GOAL:	GOAL:	GOAL:
HOW:	HOW:	HOW:
WHO:	WHO:	WHO:
WHEN:	WHEN:	WHEN:

Appendix 5

FACT SHEET

There is both good and challenging news for African-American women's health. We can advocate for our own health and wellness and change the disproportionate numbers from death and disease to stories of vibrant life. What we can do:

Mobilize to share your stories and have your voices heard in collective advocacy efforts calling for more targeted resources and funding. http://www.bwhi.org

> Black Americans are markedly more religious on a variety of measures than the U.S. population as a whole. http://blackdemographics.com/culture/religion/
>
> African-American women are increasingly using complementary therapies, such as massage therapy, meditation, yoga, and Reiki (energy work) to improve health.
>
> Along with general trends for America's population, the African American or Black population is living longer. http://www.aoa.gov/Aging_Statistics/minority_aging/Facts-on-Black-Elderly-plain_format.aspx
>
> Nearly 50% of African-American women are aware of the signs and symptoms of a heart attack.

However . . .

- Diabetes disproportionately affects African Americans at a rate nearly double that of White Americans. Nearly 6% of African American men and 8% of African American women have this disease.

- Battery against women accounts for more injuries against women than car accidents, rape, and muggings combined.

- Cigarette smoking accounts for one-third of all 30% deaths from heart disease. A woman who smokes and takes birth control pills

Live Healthy & Be Well - Hilda R. Davis

is ten times more likely to suffer a heart attack and twenty times more likely to have a stroke compared with a woman who does neither.

• Hypertension, high blood pressure, is twice as high in the Black population than in the White population. It is found in most African Americans. It relates directly to heart disease as well as stroke, diabetes, kidney disease, and blindness.

I am thinking. . .

• What thoughts come to your mind when faced with these difficult statistics? Does it make you want to change any health behaviors?

• Studies show that negative health statistics do not result in increased screenings and improved health outcomes. What helps you get your health screenings?

Getting information is a good thing. Always ask questions of your health care provider. Check out all information to make sure it makes sense for your life and health.

RESOURCES

Books

Body and Soul: The Black Women's Guide to Physical Health and Emotional Well-Being. Linda Villarosa, editor. Harper Collins, 1994.

Girlfriend to Girlfriend: Everyday Wisdom and Affirmations from the Sister Circle. Julia A. Boyd. Dutton Press, 1995.

Good Health for African Americans. Barbara Dixon. Crown Trade Books, 1994

In the Company of My Sisters: Black Women and Self-Esteem. Julia Boyd. Penguin, 1993.

Just A Sister Away: A Womanist Vision of Women's Relationships in the Bible. Renita J. Weems. Innisfree Press, 1988.

Lay My Burden Down: Unraveling Suicide and the Mental Health Crisis Among African-Americans. Alvin Poussaint, M.D. and Amy Alexander. Beacon Press, 2000.

Natural Health for African Americans. Marcellus A. Walker, M.D. and Kenneth B. Singleton, M.D. Warner Books, 1999.

Showing Mary: How Women Can Share Prayers, Wisdom, and the Blessings of God. Renita J. Weems. Warner Books, 2002.

Sisters of the Yam: Black Women and Self-Recovery. bell hooks. South End Press,1993

Staying Strong: Reclaiming the Wisdom of African-American Healing. Sara Lomax Reese and Kirk Johnson. Avon Books, 1999.

Women's Bodies, Women's Wisdom: Creating Physical and Emotional Health and Healing. Christiane Northrup, M.D. Bantam Books, 1998

Online Resources

Black Women's Health Imperative — http://www.bwhi.org
Black Women's Health — www.blackwomenshealth.org
Office on Women's Health: — www.womenshealth.gov
American Holistic Nurses Association — www.ahna.org
Health Wisdom for Women — www.drnorthrup.com
Black Women's Magazine — http://www.heartandsoul.com/
Church Health Center — http://www.churchhealthcenter.org/
World Research Foundation — www.envirolink.org
   For a sustainable environment
Guided imagery audiotapes: Health Journeys — www.healthjourneys.com

Nutrition

Black Health Matters — http://blackhealthmatters.com/
Healthy Eating — www.cdc.gov/healthyweight/healthy_eating/

Organizations

Balm in Gilead Faith-Based HIV Advocacy — www.balmingilead.org
Black Mental Health — http://www.blackmentalhealthnet.com/
American Heart Association — www.heart.org
National Alliance for Mental Illness — www.nami.org
National Heart, Lung, and Blood Institute — www.nhlbi.nih.gov
American Cancer Society — www.cancer.org
Susan G. Komen Breast Cancer Foundation — www.komen.org
American Lupus Foundation of America — www.lupus.org
American Diabetes Association — www.diabetes.org
The Alzheimer's Disease Education — www.nia.nih.gov/alzheimers/
publication/alzheimers-disease-fact-sheet

National Association of Area Agencies
 on Aging (info on home healthcare) — www.n4a.org

National Council on Aging — www.ncoa.org

Social Media — http://socialmediatoday.com/

Faith and Social Media — http://www.faithandsocialmedia.com/

REFERENCES

Boyd, Julia. *Girlfriend to Girlfriend: Everyday Wisdom and Affirmations from the Sister Circle.* Dutton Books, 1995.

Cleage, Pearl. *What Looks Like Crazy: on an ordinary day.* Avon Books, 1997.

Collier, Andrea King and Willard V. Edwards *The Black Woman's Guide To Black Men's Health.* Warner Wellness , 2007.

Davis, Hilda R. *An Ethic of Resistance: Choosing Life in Health Messages for African- American Women.* Journal of Religion and Health: Volume 50, Issue 2 (2011), Page 219.

Gandy, Debrena Jackson. *Sacred Pampering Principles: An African-American Woman's Guide to Self-care and Inner Renewal.* William Morrow, 1998.

Harper, A. Breeze. *Sistah Vegan: Food, Identity, Health, and Society.* Lantern Books, 2010.

Hoytt, Eleanor Hinton and Hilary Beard. *Health First!: The Black Woman's Wellness Guide.* Smiley Books, 2012

Mitchell, Pamela. *The 10 Lawsof Career Re-Invention: Essential Survival Skills for Any Economy.* Penquin Group, 2010.

Neal-Barnett, Angela. Soothe Your Nerves: *The Black Woman's Guide to Understanding and Overcoming Anxiety, Panic, and Fear.* Fireside, 2003.

Taylor, Jewel Diamond. *Success Gems: Your Personal Motivational Success Guide.* Quiet Time, 1999.

William, Terrie. *Black Pain: It Just Looks Like We Are Not Hurting.* Scribner, 2008

Winbush Riley, Dorothy. *Black Women in the Image of God.* Pilgrim Press, 1999.

NOTES

NOTES

NOTES

NOTES

NOTES

NOTES

81416007R00064

Made in the USA
Lexington, KY
16 February 2018